D1590214

NAVIGATING TOWARD ADULTHOOD

A Theology of Ministry with Adolescents

Theresa A. O'Keefe

Paulist Press
New York / Mahwah, NJ

Cover art: *King Melchior Sailing to the Holy Land* (c. 1445–50) by Pesellino. (Tempera, oil, and gold on panel.) A small fleet accompanies one of the three kings who, according to Christian tradition, brought gifts to the infant Jesus. King Melchior sits enthroned in the stern of a sailing ship, his robes and crown decorated with gold leaf. A fifteenth-century hunting party and two monks appear in the foreground, perhaps to make this scriptural scene more relevant to a fifteenth-century audience. The image ends abruptly on the left side; the panel was cut down at some point after it was removed from its original location. Image courtesy of the Clark Institute, Williamstown, Massachusetts, USA.

Cover design by Lightly Salted Graphics
Book design by Lynn Else

Library of Congress Cataloging-in-Publication Data
Names: O'Keefe, Theresa A., author.
Title: Navigating toward adulthood : a theology of ministry with adolescents / Theresa A. O'Keefe.
Description: New York : Paulist Press, 2018. | Includes bibliographical references and index.
Identifiers: LCCN 2018014068 (print) | LCCN 2018036147 (ebook) | ISBN 9781587687709 (ebook) | ISBN 9780809153985 (pbk. : alk. paper)
Subjects: LCSH: Church work with young adults—Catholic Church. | Church work with teenagers—Catholic Church.
Classification: LCC BX2347.8.Y64 (ebook) | LCC BX2347.8.Y64 O34 2018 (print) | DDC 259/.23—dc23
LC record available at https://lccn.loc.gov/2018014068

ISBN 978-0-8091-5398-5 (paperback)
ISBN 978-1-58768-770-9 (e-book)

Published by Paulist Press
997 Macarthur Boulevard
Mahwah, New Jersey 07430

www.paulistpress.com

Printed and bound in the
United States of America

Contents

Acknowledgments

This work has been years in the making. Not simply because I am a slow writer, which I am, but because I am also a slow thinker. It took time to refine my thoughts and determine what I really needed to say. That was not time spent mulling in solitude, but in conversation with several valuable interlocutors. For them I am deeply grateful.

First, I acknowledge my graduate students who have taken my course, "The Practice of Ministry with Youth and Young Adults," over the years. That course has been the breeding and testing ground for the ideas in this book. In more recent years, these students have read draft chapters and helped me stay on point. I especially thank Michelle Keefe and Tony Kryzmarzyk for their very close and critical reading of early chapters, and Peter Fay for early research assistance.

A value of teaching at Boston College's School of Theology and Ministry is the strong collegiality among the faculty. I acknowledge my colleagues who gave guidance to my work from their own disciplines: Christopher Frechette, Catherine Mooney, and Ernesto Valiente. I also acknowledge my dean, Mark Massa, and department chairs, Thomas Groome and Jane Regan, for allowing space in my teaching and service so that I could work on the manuscript.

Finally, I thank Cynthia Cameron for closely reading every chapter as the project came to an end; Susannah Singer, my dear friend and colleague, for her great support throughout; and my wonderful Irene, who supports me in all ways.

Introduction

I have had the good fortune of teaching and researching in adolescent faith for many years. I have also had the opportunity to work with adolescents, young and old, and with ministerial leaders and educators working with this age demographic. Over the years I have been prompted to ask, what is going on in adolescence, or more specifically, how is God at work in this time of life? This book is my effort to answer that question.

This is a book in four parts. In part 1, chapter 1, we establish the book's argument, namely that the project of adolescence—the growth from childhood to adulthood—is to find one's place in the world and involves multiple relational and interpretive tasks. In chapters 2 and 3, we identify cultural factors that make the relational and interpretive tasks of adolescents difficult. We identify the dominant cultural narrative of individualism, set within a market-based economy, and the accumulated social practices of isolation, as both contributing to the separation of adolescents from adults. We then consider how the practices of digital technology negatively impact an adolescent's ability to develop and grow relationships. In part 2, we argue for the social nature of adulthood, offering, first, a definition of adulthood as being responsible within the context of relationships. Thus, adolescence *is* the time to learn to be responsible within the context of relationships. We then describe how the social surroundings shape how the adolescent understands himself and his sense of value. In part 3, we name adolescence as the optimal life stage for the transformation from an instrumental to a relational engagement with the world. We observe the cognitive development happening throughout this life stage, such that the adolescent can see and value relationships in a way that is different from the instrumental perspective of childhood. We then advocate for robust relationships as those which prompt the transformation. Finally, in part 4, we consider the church's response. We focus on how Christian narratives, embodied in the lives of real people, communicate a horizon upon which adolescents may interpret their lives. We close with the suggestion that robust relationships and relational practices support the development of the relational and interpretive tasks of adolescence. Throughout our inquiry is a theological argument identifying the constant presence and movement of God's grace in the transformation of adolescents.

My brother once likened the shift to adulthood as that of moving from a passenger's seat to the driver's seat of a car. To be in the driver's seat, he suggested, involves making decisions for oneself, to take on responsibility for one's life, and for the lives of others. It is a rich image for the movement toward adult agency. Yet the metaphor relies upon presumptions: there are roads from which to choose; the ground underneath does not move; one can depend on an engine to power progress and brakes to slow down. Furthermore, driving is a solo operation, which seldom improves with the input from passengers.

The metaphor is fine for what it suggests about agency and direction, but the "road of life" is not so clearly mapped. A few years ago, I learned the art of sailing, which offers a richer metaphor for adulthood.

First, sailing is a highly interpretive task. There are few clear "signposts" in sailing, such as channel markers and lighthouses. However, there are many signs that the sailor only learns to read with experience, such as changes in wind speed and strength of current. In fact, making any progress in a sailboat depends on the sailor's ability to interpret the constant flux of wind and current. The sailor, like the adult, needs to work with what is available in a context, over which she has no control, but with which she can, and must, make progress. Her success depends on her ability to accurately interpret her world to make progress.

Second, sailing, like adulthood, calls for cooperation. Few adult responsibilities are accomplished alone, whether work, family, or social. While some sailing can be accomplished alone, sailing anything but the smallest boats generally requires the contribution of others. Sailing benefits from the energy and insights of the crew; it depends on others, some whose experience is greater, and some lesser.

Introduction

Finally, like adulthood, sailing is largely learned in the doing. Books and formal classrooms can be helpful, but sailing is best learned incrementally, on the water, among and from experienced sailors— and it is never fully mastered, never perfected, and always new.

The metaphor of sailing will illustrate the following discussion. I hope you find it helpful.

Part One

LOST AT SEA

As a child vacationing with my family on Cape Cod, I loved to watch the ocean waves breaking on the beach as a storm approached. It was wonderful to see the power, beauty, and variety expressed in those waves. I was mesmerized. I would sit on the bench at the top of the seawall with my father, but as the air got cooler and the rain became heavier, he would suggest we return to the cottage. It was hard to turn away, and I remember thinking to myself that I would leave as soon as the waves stopped. However, as soon as the thought became conscious, I would laugh to myself, thinking, *The waves are not going to stop.* Inside me for the next few moments, I would experience a back-and-forth between the sense that I would wait until the waves were finished and the recognition that they never would be finished. The difficulty of turning away was inspired by my fascination with the waves and the feeling that I did not want to miss out on anything by turning back to the cottage.

Similarly, we can be fascinated with the waves of constant activity in the social context of the United States in the early twenty-first century. As deep as that desire for stability and clarity may be, the reality is that our social worlds are always experiencing flux. Rather than turn away from the constant flux, it is helpful to examine the changing social worlds in which adolescents, young adults, and even faith communities live, for it is in that world that ministry happens. As we examine the wider social worlds in which adolescents and young adults are growing to maturity and pay attention to how they are reacting to those worlds, we gain a better sense of the factors that contribute to the challenges of growing to maturity today.

1

In this first part of the book, we identify factors of life in the United States as they affect our ability to recognize and deepen relationships. These are global factors, meaning they impact adolescents at large, even if the impact is felt differently in specific circumstances and contexts. Variables such as wealth or poverty, immigration status, geography—rural, suburban, or urban—ethnicity, and race may alter an individual's experience of these factors but they are pervasive. In chapter 2, I investigate cultural messages of independence and social structures of isolation, including the day-to-day interaction with an expanding number of people. In chapter 3, I look to the relational practices of digital technology and the impact of those practices on initiating and deepening relationships. I suggest those practices may, in fact, deepen the divides among us rather than foster relationships.

Just as the Spirit of God hovers over the abyss in the Creation account (Gen 1:2), God continues to hover today. Convinced that God creates out of nothing (*ex nihilo*), I believe this flux we experience has its ultimate source in God and that God's abundance surrounds us, full of grace and possibility. This is not to deny the reality of sin and evil, but to say we should neither confuse flux and the abyss with sin nor correlate stability with evidence of grace. In fact, evil has sometimes been able to spread unquestioned because of humanity's preference for stability and the desire for good and evil to be clearly labeled. While the disorder may be disheartening amid its effects, our faith moves us to be confident in God's presence within the flux. Hearing God's voice during stormy conditions can be difficult. In addition to that, we are not sitting up on the seawall watching the waves from a safe distance. Instead, like Peter and the apostles, we are in a small craft on the surface of the water, buffeted by the wind and water (Matt 14:24). Amid the storms of our lives, we must remember that God is greater than the storm and that, even here, we are held and not lost.

1

The Project of Adolescence

S ometimes we talk about *adolescents* as if they are alien life-forms or *adolescence* as a dark and mysterious life stage; each feeling more like something foreign, unfamiliar, and even frightening. Considering these impressions, ministry with adolescents is frequently regarded as work reserved for those special and intrepid folk willing to travel into unknown territories. The irony of these perceptions is that all of us— at least the readers of this book—have passed through that life stage and have been that alien. Consequently, it should not seem so foreign. Even though most adults have strong and vivid memories of their time as adolescents, it can be hard to make sense of what was going on amid those experiences. Or perhaps because of their vividness and seeming complexity, the overall arch is obscured.[1] In the early twenty-first century, there are certain phenomena affecting adolescents and young adults that add to the confusion and further cloud the landscape. Diverse voices name and attribute these phenomena differently. Many refer to an extended adolescence, pointing to the failure of North American youth to settle into the markers of adulthood, such as long-term employment, marriage, and becoming independent of parents;[2] while others point to an increase among youth in risk factors such as depression, suicide, and binge drinking.[3] Still others look to concerns regarding the decline in religious practice and belonging.[4] Of alarming concern is the increasing number of mass shootings, particularly school shootings, perpetuated by older adolescents but frequently victimizing

3

other adolescents and children.[5] Ministry to and with adolescents at this juncture seems all the more pressing. Yet without a clear sense of the "direction" of adolescence, ministry efforts with and to adolescents can seem like wandering in the dark; it hopes to affect good or at least to avoid falling into pits.

As obscured as it may become, the major "project" of adolescence is simple. Through the lengthy maturation process of adolescence — starting with puberty and ending by the late twenties — the growing human becomes able to figure out where and how she fits in the world.[6] She is called to move from the unselfconscious place of childhood to the more self-aware world of adulthood. She comes to know who she is, whose she is, where she stands, and why it all matters, so that she might contribute her life to that world in a meaningful way.[7] This "project" is composed of interrelated, overlapping, but distinct "tasks," all of which happen with some concurrency, and all of which depend on each other to come to fruition. Each task requires the cognitive development that comes with adolescence but is not inevitable with the passing of time. Each task needs prompting, appropriate challenge, and support to become actualized. The first task is for her to *discover herself as a person*, differently from how she saw herself as a child. The second is that she becomes able to see *others as persons*, complex and distinct from herself. And the third is to recognize the *relationships* that exist between her and them. But even these three tasks require the development of a variety of relational "practices" such as listening, growing in sympathy and empathy, perspective taking, long-range planning, imagining consequence, and so on. These tasks of self-seeing and relating — initiated in the early teen years with clumsy steps and little nuance — in time, with prompting, support, and practice, take on refinement in the early to mid-twenties, such that the individual develops a relational sensibility and can stand more confidently as an adult in the world.

Finally, a fourth task for the maturing adolescent is interpretive. Discovering her place in the world requires the adolescent to make sense of her life and her world. Her maturation toward adulthood demands more than simply increasing her fund of technical knowledge; rather, it demands of her a new capacity to read and interpret the surrounding cultural narratives and practices such that she can participate with new agency in that culture. As she matures, she looks up from the immediate to scan the horizon for signs and meaning.

Through witnessing and participating in the surrounding cultural narratives and practices, she discovers what the world expects of her and who she is at the center of those expectations; she learns to live into what is appropriate and possible for her. Thus, her interpretation and response to the world are at the heart of her maturation process.

Discovering Oneself as a Person

Whereas a child seems so clear to herself, an adolescent, newly able to see and acknowledge her inner life, becomes confused, empowered, and surprised at what she finds within herself—a unique person with thoughts, feelings, interests, and viewpoints. Thus, the task of self-discovery is initiated with the growth of self-consciousness. This self-discovery process is further complicated by the other tasks, her growing awareness of the personhood of others and her relationship with them. In effect, because of the discovery of herself as a unique person, she is trying to figure out her relationship with the world and with these others. Therefore, her perceptions of them and of their judgments of her become deeply influential in her self-concept. Questions of identity, vocation, purpose, desirability, belonging, and romance emerge. This task of self-discovery is both mysterious and complex. It is complex because each question is interwoven with the next question, and all implicate and are implicated by the other people in her life. The process is also mysterious because, in discovering who she is, she enters a deep mystery: her familiar yet unknowable self. That discovery can be both exhilarating and frightening. This one task that she is invited to accomplish through adolescence—her self-discovery as a unique and specific person—is part of the project of finding her place in the world.

According to theologian John Zizioulas, the discovery of one's personhood is no small discovery. For it is in our personhood, he claims, that we are made in the "image of God" (Gen 1:27). Reflecting on the fourth-century Cappadocian Fathers, who argued for God's being in three persons—Father, Son, and Spirit—Zizioulas claims the anthropological consequences of their trinitarian theology is to affirm the personhood of the individual human. Zizioulas distinguishes our *nature* (*what* we are) from our *being* (*how* we are) to identify in what ways we are like God and unlike God. He argues that we are unlike

God in our nature. Human nature (the human *what*), which is created by God, is unlike God's nature (God's *what*), which is uncreated. Zizioulas writes, "The 'natural' characteristics of human nature, such as dividedness—and hence individuation leading to decomposition and finally death—are all aspects of human 'substance' and determine the human being as far as its nature is concerned."[8] In fact, he asserts, as individual humans, our nature makes us indistinguishable from other humans; each of us is just one among billions. However, we can be like God in our being (*how* we are), how we relate to others. He argues we are drawn out of the vast sea of humanity and discover our unique personhood in the experience of receiving and giving love— when someone looks at us lovingly and says, "Yes, you." Zizioulas argues that *how* being a person, giving oneself freely in loving relationship to another person, is what makes us in God's image. "The 'image of God' in man has precisely to do with this *how*, not with the *what* man is." Zizioulas continues, "Living…according to the image of God means living in the way God exists, that is, as an image of God's personhood."[9] God's *how* is as a communion of persons: "none of the three persons can be conceived without reference to the other two."[10] Thus to be a person, according to Zizioulas, means three things: to be freely giving of oneself (not compelled by anything outside oneself); to be in communion, in relationship; and to be unique among humans in that free gift of self. This discovery of our personhood only happens in relationships of love. He writes,

> It is the other and our relationship with him that gives us our identity, our otherness, making us "who we are", i.e. persons; for by being an inseparable part of a relationship that matters ontologically we emerge as *unique* and *irreplaceable* entities. This, therefore, is what accounts for our being ourselves and not someone else: our personhood. It is in this that the "reason," the *logos* of our being lies: in the relationship of love that makes us unique and irreplaceable *for another*.[11]

For Zizioulas, we can never be a person, in general. The particularities of our relationships of love with another draw us out of our general human nature to be a *person for* someone else. Furthermore, our personhood is never at the expense of another person, as in a zero-sum

6

equation. Rather, grounded in the ecstatic personhood of God, each person grows in relation to another's growth. It is in our relationships of love that we become unique and irreplaceable as we are being drawn by the other's love. We become ecstatic, freely and generously giving ourselves in love. Thus, such relationships are essential for the discovery of personhood.

In Relation to Others

For the adolescent to see herself as a person, a couple things need to be in place. First, she needs to develop the cognitive capacities of ideation and self-consciousness, whereby the adolescent can say to herself, "I think I am someone." Of course, her statement usually arises more as a question or a hope than as a claim of fact. Such self-seeing opens new horizons for self-understanding and relationality within the adolescent. For her to develop an appreciation of herself as a person of value and consequence, the second thing she needs, as Zizioulas asserts, are relationships with credible others outside herself to affirm her as such. Yet it is not enough that they affirm her; she needs to recognize their affirmation as authentic and as having value in the world. Their affirmation needs to count for something so that she can begin to count herself as something. Thus, she needs relationships with significant, trustworthy others to see and value her for whom she is to them. If not readily supplied by trustworthy relationships, she may desperately search for affirmation elsewhere; likewise, she may be pursued by untrustworthy agents looking to draw her in for their benefit, not hers.[12]

As she comes to see herself with greater complexity, the second task becomes possible: she can recognize others as more mysterious than previously seen. Romantic partners are not just "people who reflect well on me." Friends are more than "people with whom I do stuff." Parents are no longer just "suppliers of groceries and other needs." Rather than simply extensions of herself, in time each becomes a unique person with his or her own interests, hopes, and desires. They too become persons who cannot be categorized and contained within her self-interest. By recognizing the personhood of others, she grows beyond the *instrumental* seeing that aided her through childhood—whereby she engages with others for their exchange value—toward a *relational* sensibility—an appreciation of others as persons with whom she is in relationship.

Yet the adolescent's recognition of others' personhood and the shift toward a relational sense is not automatic. It comes, in part, because others demand that she recognize and respond to them as persons of value who require respect and care. If she is to listen to their demands on her, they need to be people she cannot easily dismiss or ignore (at least not for long); the connections must have some extrinsic value for the adolescent. Without prompts from others, it is likely that the instrumental perspective she gained in childhood will only persist and become savvier over time; she will continue to see herself as the center of her world and others as aids or impediments to her interests. Thus, significant relationships provide the *curriculum* and the *class-room* as well as the *motivation* for her learning, and are necessary for her to recognize the world outside herself. These significant others shift from their instrumental purpose to become unique, valuable, and irreplaceable persons. The relationships gain an intrinsic value for the adolescent such that the adolescent begins to work for the good of the relationship and the other. Theologian Catherine LaCugna writes, "To say someone is a person is to acknowledge that we cannot exactly and completely define him or her."[13] Once begun, the ability to recognize the personhood of another human is a never-ending pursuit. The growing adolescent will be called to do it throughout the rest of her life, extending personhood first to those close at hand for whom she cares, and then in time and with prodding, as Jesus commanded, even to the stranger and enemy (Matt 5:44).

Located on a Meaningful Horizon

For the adolescent, finding her place in the world is not an act of creating her place and purpose out of thin air. Rather, it is an interpretive task whereby she makes sense of the world in which she finds herself and thus makes sense of herself. Developmental theorist Erik Erikson notes that, as the adolescent matures, she gains the ability to think conceptually, thematically, and historically, thus imagining her life as part of a landscape greater than herself.[14] Embedded within the practices and narratives of cultural spaces—family, education, employment, religion, and the wider culture—the adolescent discovers the meaning of those spaces and how she fits within them.[15] While many elements of culture do not purport to point to ultimate ends, all narratives and practices point to some ontological purpose whether those ends are explicitly named or not.[16] These cultural spaces shape her imagination, implicitly and explicitly. She begins to infer what the cultural messages intend for her life, thus providing horizons of ultimate meaning upon which she finds herself located. Philosopher Hans-Georg Gadamer describes "horizon" in this way:

> The horizon is the range of vision that includes everything that can be seen from a particular vantage point....A person who has no horizon does not see far enough and hence overvalues what is nearest to him. On the other hand, "to have a horizon" means not being limited to what is nearby but being able to see beyond it. A person who has a horizon knows the relative significance of everything within this horizon, whether it is near or far, great or small.[17]

Horizon is a useful metaphor in that it provides a way of communicating a view of a goal as well as the adolescent's location vis-à-vis that goal.

However, through a variety of means, contemporary culture communicates to the maturing adolescent that she should make her own sense of the world and of her life; she should name her identity unencumbered by cultural norms, ultimate ends, or explicit direction. Furthermore, to restrict her options is to restrict her freedom of choice.[18] Such messages suggest that meaning making happens within a vacuum or without drawing from a surrounding social world. Such messages are unhelpful and potentially deceitful. They are unhelpful because it suggests to adults and adolescents that the adolescent does not need help interpreting her world or making sense of her identity; she should be encouraged to figure it out on her own. One result of these messages is that adults back off, not wishing to impose ideas on the adolescent; another result is that the adolescent does not seek out help, expecting she should be able to figure it out for herself.[19] These messages are deceitful because they suggest that it does not matter how the adolescent makes sense of things, all possibilities are equally valid and laudatory.[20] Either way, so much adolescent anxiety is generated by the misfit between the adolescent's understanding of herself and the world's expectations for her. In fact, it is possibly the unaided effort to bridge the chasm between what the world expects and the adolescent's sense of self that contributes to the extension of adolescence for so many.

Acknowledged or not, the surrounding social world *is* what frames the adolescent's sense of self. Philosopher Alasdair MacIntyre writes, "For the story of my life is always embedded in the story of those communities from which I derive my identity. I am born with a past; and to try to cut myself off from that past…is to deform my present relationships."[21] If we acknowledge the role of the social surround in shaping the adolescent's sense of meaning and purpose, then we can attest to the importance of attending to shaping that surround, even though we might do it differently for adolescents than we would for children. Part of ministry to adolescents then is to share the Christian tradition as an expansive and meaningful horizon upon which the adolescent might imagine her life and worth. Through our narratives and practices, we can invite, encourage, and assist the adolescent to regularly look up from that which is immediately in front of her and prompt her imagination to see her life and all life as meaningful, worthy, and full of graceful possibility. While she will spend her time amid other social worlds, she may be better equipped to carry the Christian narratives and practices to those other worlds.

Ministerial Response

Considering the "project" of adolescence, I suggest ministry to and with adolescents—in all its variety and contexts—is to assist in the adolescent's various and connected tasks of interpretation, imagination, and discovery: of himself as a person of unique value; of the personhood of others; of his relationships to them and the world. It is also to assist in growing the relational practices—both the challenges and graces of living with love—that support those tasks. Ministry includes helping him imagine himself and others within the horizon of his relationship with God. Stated differently, it is to assist the adolescent in recognizing his life as a unique gift he receives from God, and that his life is a unique gift to be given by him for the life of the world. This is accomplished by sharing a meaningful horizon and the companionship of reliable others who invite him to join them in the practices and narratives of interpretation and action.

A GIFT TO BE RECEIVED

Part of the confusion of adolescence is that the adolescent is coming to discover more within himself, more than he ever recognized before. New energy, interests, ideas, attractions, emotions, desires, hopes—even his body and hormones—can come as a surprise. These pieces of himself cannot be easily defined or understood, and he appears much more complicated to himself than he seemed as a child. Furthermore, his childhood perspective that life *just is* comes to be replaced by questions of *why life is*. And with that recognition come questions of the adolescent's place and purpose. It is exactly this ability to see himself that enables him and calls him to see his life on a horizon of meaning greater than himself. However, coming to this capacity today, in a world marked by so much diversity and contradiction, means that there is no guarantee he will perceive that horizon as meaningful or ultimately hopeful. That horizon may be perceived as empty, wherein he finds himself alone. That horizon may be perceived as a place of competition whereby he conceives himself as a commodity seeking exchange value.[22] That horizon may be perceived as a place of multiple, equal options, thus rendering his choice meaningless.[23] Or that horizon may offer only one legitimate vision that, he perceives, saves some and damns others. Even if he were baptized into the Christian community, it cannot be presumed that he will recognize this wider horizon as God, who calls him forth in love.

Thus, an essential ministry of the Christian community is to provide a narrative and practices that help the adolescent interpret his life on a horizon of meaning, hope, and purpose, whereby God rushes to meet the adolescent as he is. This claim rests on a belief that the human person—like all creation—is made by and in relationship with God. God is not one thing among other things seeking allegiance, but the mystery that is the source and heart of all life and being, outside of which nothing exists. The human person is never not in relationship with God, even if that relationship is unacknowledged by the human. Nor does the relationship end with creation, like a clock set in motion and left to itself to wind down its days. Rather, it is God's very self that is communicated somehow in and through the human life created and

11

sustained in God. As the adolescent becomes able to see himself, he can begin to make sense of his life, to locate himself within and in relationship with the world. He can see himself within his experiences and make sense of them; he gains the capacity to examine his life and wonder about wider meaning and purpose.

Theologian Karl Rahner was instrumental in placing the knowing human subject at the center of theological discourse while affirming human "access" to the transcendent mystery that Christians name God. Rahner wrote of *transcendental experience* as the "subject's openness to the unlimited expanse of all possible reality" whereby the limitless and the immediate are copresent in experience.[24] Thus the human person can open himself to recognize the deep mystery at the heart of life, placing himself amid a vast framework of meaning. This attention, Rahner claimed, is what brings the person to "the threshold of becoming a religious person,"[25] by which Rahner meant that the person comes to recognize a *telos*, an "end," beyond himself that directs and inspires his life. His life is not self-referential but directed toward infinite mystery. Yet Rahner admitted that a person "can always choose to accept this infinite question only as a thorn in the side of his knowledge and his mastery and control" and thus limit his perspective to the immediate and personal.[26] Theologian Edward Hahnenberg writes,

> For Rahner, the infinite horizon of the human person is nothing less than the mystery of God. What grounds our knowing (as well as our choosing and our loving) is neither an unending emptiness nor absolute Being. It is the God of Jesus Christ. God is the horizon that opens up the landscape and encircles our lives, calling us forward even as it continually recedes before us.[27]

If the adolescent is fortunate enough to come to this wondering within the Christian community, he may be given the language, narrative, practices, and companionship that will help him discern his life within the presence and movement of God.

Frequently, the contemporary adolescent may try to sequester himself, holing up in his bedroom or some such private space, to come to some clarity out of sight of others. Or he might reach out to anonymous others through digital media, to test out ideas and find validation without fear of embarrassing himself. But his private effort remains isolated. For he is attempting an interpretive process; this requires the feedback of reliable others for him to discover who he is and where he fits in among others. He will need affirmation from trustworthy others to make sense of, integrate, and evaluate all these aspects of himself. It will take time and interaction with others to discover what endures, what is passing, what is important, what is valuable, and how all fit together within him. In time, and it *will* take time, he will come to see himself with greater distinction and clarity, but it will require ongoing interactions with others to accomplish.

What the Christian community can do is help the adolescent begin to examine and interpret his life so as to see its value in light of God's presence and call. The community, in its practices and presence, helps the adolescent learn to see, as Rahner writes, "that holy mystery is present not only as a remoteness and distance which situates us in our finiteness, but also in the mode of an absolute and forgiving closeness."[28] The community offers a means for interpreting life. In the mystery that is his own life, the adolescent can come to appreciate more deeply the mystery that is God. For him to receive his life as given by God is the entryway of his salvation. As Rahner claims,

> For the true theological notion of salvation does not mean a future situation which befalls a person unexpectedly like something from outside....Nor does it mean something bestowed on him only on the basis of a moral judgment. It means rather the final and definitive validity of a person's true self-understanding and true self-realization in freedom before God by the fact that he accepts his own self as it is disclosed and offered to him in the choice of transcendence as interpreted in freedom.[29]

To assist the adolescent in doing so, the Christian community, as a communion of saints, provides the practices of companionship, encouragement, affirmation, and guidance in discerning God's word and movement in the life of the adolescent. It helps him train his imagination and ground his experience, so that he might recognize himself as loved by and beloved of God. Hahnenberg writes, "God calls us forward to respond by carrying forward our deepest identity—to be saints by being ourselves."[30] Thus, the adolescent is companioned and invited by the communion of saints to see the saint within himself.

A GIFT TO BE GIVEN

Another ministry of the Christian community to the adolescent is to encourage her in the task of recognizing the personhood of others and responding in relationship. This is done both through the members themselves inviting and challenging her to be in relationship with them, and likewise inviting and challenging her to recognize the personhood of those in the wider world who need recognition and care. For the gift of the adolescent's personhood is not for her to keep to herself. Rather, it is meant to call her out to be present to others. It is to be given as a gift to the world.

Just as she can learn to look for and be attentive to the presence of God within her own life, the Christian community can prompt her imagination to acknowledge the presence of God within another and within the created order. Through developing practices of attending and relating, she can come to recognize the unique value of another, and move out to that other in love, whether that other is family, friend, romantic other, classmate, stranger on the street, or a distant victim of war. Hahnenberg writes, "The 'essence' of Christianity lies precisely in its openness to the other."[31] And later he writes, "We grow in this openness to God—who is *the Other*—precisely by growing in openness to others."[32] Yet, giving herself as gift is not a task she accomplishes once for all time, like a requirement for the sacrament of confirmation or the outcome of a single immersion experience. Rather it is a stance of openness to and caring for the other that she learns to take on and practice over time and in varied circumstances. Considered in this way, it becomes important to ponder where and how such an attitude of openness is learned and practiced.

Learning the wide-ranging practices of attending and relating to the other cannot be limited to the adolescent's relationships with age peers or parents. Nor is teaching these practices a job reserved for the professional experts, like youth ministers, theology teachers, campus ministers, or chaplains; while they may each play a vital role in coordinating and creating the environment for such relationships, it is unlikely that they will develop a robust relational bond with every adolescent in their care. Rather, the "teachers" must include others from the wider pool of potential connections surrounding an adolescent, including extended family members, parents of friends, family friends, neighbors, school stakeholders, and church congregants. Each

14

of these offer perspectives on living in the world, but they also present a potential relationship that recognizes and responds to the adolescent as a person and calls her to recognize and respond to them as persons.[33]

When we consider the project and tasks of adolescence in this broad way, we begin to appreciate the role the wider communion of saints can play in the ministry with and to adolescents. Theologian Elizabeth Johnson writes of the communion of saints as an "evocative symbol" of the Christian church.[34] While our imagination may move first to those named and honored in the church's liturgical cycle, the communion of saints comprises a broader community, including the many "friends of God and prophets" currently living. Johnson writes,

> [The] communion of saints is comprised first of all of the current generation of living Christians who respond to the promptings of the Spirit and follow the way of Jesus in the world. In the circumstances of their own historical time and place, these women and men try to be faithful friends of and courageous prophets, taking seriously the invitation to love God and neighbor and pouring good purpose into their lives.[35]

The communion of saints is a living community that provides lively and inspired companionship in our congregations. They are the people with whom we worship, sing, and pray, provide outreach, study, celebrate the sacramental life, and enjoy fellowship. They are both models and companions "who respond to the promptings of the Spirit." Along with these living, the communion of saints includes the "cloud of witnesses" (Heb 12:1), named and unnamed, who have gone before us. Johnson suggests that through our narrative and practices, the "saints on earth have access to the company of these saints in heaven through memory and hope."[36] Beyond those historic figures recognized in the larger church, the communion of saints also includes those personally dear whose memory remains a source of solace and courage for our lives here and now: deceased family and friends.

The communion of saints, both living and dead, manifests in diverse ways how we are called to receive our lives from God and give our lives to the world. They serve as companions and models to adolescents in living faithfully and courageously in the world. The stories of their lives, with loving, courageous, and perhaps prophetic acts, inspire adolescents to imagine and interpret their lives as gifts for the world. The saints also serve as teachers and copractitioners of the various relational practices found within the Christian tradition; practices include prayer and worship, proclamation and study of Scripture, the sacramental life, service to those in need, and critical and prophetic engagement with the world. All of these practiced with an eye to "follow the way of Jesus in the world" instruct the adolescent and invite them to join them in practicing the love of God and openness to neighbor.[37]

Offering a Horizon and a Community of Interpretation

The central narrative of the Christian community is that God is the source of all life—even the adolescent's—and that God gives Godself freely in love, as love, calling all creation to participate in love through receiving and giving the gift of their lives. Returning to the words of Hahnenberg, "God is the horizon that opens up the landscape and encircles [the adolescent's life], calling [him] forward even as it continually recedes before [him]."[38] This horizon holds him with care and self-giving love and draws him to see his life in relationship with all of creation on that horizon. As God is Communion, so the adolescent is called into communion—into relationship—with others and with God, so as to discover his personhood. The community, through its many practices, trains the adolescent how to be in communion, how to love God and love neighbor as himself. It trains him to open his eyes to see his life and the world as a gift given freely. The community, in its practices, teaches him to open his heart and risk giving himself compassionately to the other. These are not lessons learned in leaps and bounds or accomplished once for all time. Rather, they are learned incrementally with repetition, reminding, missteps, failure, forgiveness, reconciliation, and much practice! The community models the truth that we are never perfected—never free of mistakes—but always open to greater grace. It is within the community that the adolescent may find companions of all ages and experience to share these practices. It is within the community that he may find robust relationships that help him discover himself and his place in the world by finding his place in that community.

16

The Project of Adolescence

When children learn to sail, it is usually close to shore, in small boats like the *Optimist* (often referred to as a "bathtub with a sail"). In such situations, the young sailor has only to focus on her actions in the boat and her immediate surroundings. An able instructor is always nearby, paying attention to the wider environment, giving instruction, and guarding her safety. But in time, our young sailor will outgrow the *Opti*—literally. If she is to continue sailing, she will need to move onto a larger boat. The larger boat will make it possible—and necessary—to move beyond the shoreline and farther out to sea. Likewise, the larger vessel will bring with it an invitation and an expectation to work with other crew members, attending to the work of the boat, but also reading the conditions outside the boat and looking toward the horizon. Such is the growth of adolescence. It is an invitation into deeper waters, scanning the horizon, newly responsible to others, and working toward some meaningful pursuit. Successfully finding her place along that horizon, in the company of others, will bring her ably to the demands of adulthood.

2

Sailing Solo

There is a certain fascination with adventurers who seem to master a grand accomplishment on their own. Whether they swim from Cuba to Florida, bike across the country, or sail around the world, we admire their courage and skill. The part of the story that is frequently overlooked is how many people were required to help them do their "solo" act. Whether it is the support boats aside the swimmer, the friends and strangers along the route who offer hospitality, or the various ports of call that provided the necessary repairs, food, and company. Sailing solo is only intermittently solo. Even those attempting an ocean crossing do so from port to port with extensive preparation, with tremendous personal skill—both nautical and mechanical—and, today, with increasing dependence on technology. Otherwise, solo sailing is reserved to small crafts, sailed close to shore. Yet the solo effort is often portrayed as the height of courage, ability, and accomplishment. Such portrayals are part of a cultural narrative that proclaims that the greatest accomplishments are achieved on one's own. But these narratives promote a false vision, because they dismiss the essential role that relationships with others played in accomplishing the tasks. As such, they are misleading, for our most important accomplishments are never truly solo operations.

In this chapter, we argue that, in the contemporary United States, the combination of cultural messages of individualism and social structures of isolation has become a stumbling block for adolescent maturation to adulthood. We identify dominant cultural narratives and practices that contribute to a sense of isolation that is a felt reality for so many adolescents. In doing so, we look beyond "youth culture" to

18

the broader culture. For there are significant factors within the broader culture that impact adolescents more negatively than older adults. Furthermore, youth culture finds its power within the broader culture that allows or normalizes elements of youth culture.[1] Here we will examine briefly the conditions within the culture that discourage the development of robust relationships between adolescents and adults. These conditions have developed over decades, even centuries, but have become so normalized as to seem invisible or inconsequential.

Cultural Messages

A major cultural stumbling block to developing relationships and a relational sensibility is the presumption within current United States' culture that the human person is meant to go it alone. Cultural narratives often frame self-interest as contrary to or in competition with relationships. In *Bowling Alone*, sociologist Robert Putnam writes, "Our national myths often exaggerate the role of individual heroes and understate the importance of collective effort….[The] myth of rugged individualism continues to strike a powerful inner chord in the American psyche."[2] Similarly, Robert Bellah reports in *Habits of the Heart* that we are "in a culture that emphasizes the autonomy and self-reliance of the individual" and sees maturation into adulthood as a process of increasing "separation and individuation…[and] the all-important event of leaving home."[3] Bellah explains that the nineteenth-century message of self-reliance was promoted in "a clearly collective" context, on which it depended: "It was as a people that we acted independently and self-reliantly" through congregations, civic structures, and volunteer associations.[4] However, now valuable political and philosophical messages about the importance and value of the individual actor are no longer surrounded by the implicit social and communal givens of the eighteenth and nineteenth centuries. Without those structural and cultural givens to temper the explicit messages promoting the individual, we are left with an emaciated conception of the person in society: the individual whose rights are emphasized apart from responsibilities to others and the common good.

For more than a century, the narratives of the individual have grown accretions seeded by a consumer market, which finds a loyal consumer in the busy, distracted, and disconnected individual.[5] Thus, in the early twenty-first century, self-reliance and independence are interpreted and lived as calls for the individual to act by him- or herself in isolation, and to prefer that solo pursuit over the concerns of, or the need for, the communal. Furthermore, theologian Vincent Miller argues that contemporary consumer marketing intentionally and constantly misdirects deep human desires for connection toward fleeting and unsatisfying products and services. Thus, as busy participants in a marketplace culture, we are distracted from deeper pursuits and relationships. We are increasingly directed to interpret our life's purpose and meaning as directed toward consumption and commoditization.[6] From there, it is a short step to seeing *oneself* as a commodity within a competitive marketplace.[7]

The impact of the cultural messages of individualism and consumption are potentially greater on adolescents than on adults. As they are coming to see their social worlds and deeply desire to form relationships, they also are becoming aware of diverse cultural messages that thwart those very desires. Because this awareness is newly developing in adolescents, adolescents are, in a sense, like canaries in a coal mine, first to notice and suffer from atmospheric conditions that more mature adults may not notice. While resilient, adolescents often are more likely than mature adults to respond negatively to cultural stressors, because they have not yet gained sufficient perspective to interpret the stressors or the capacity to modulate their reactions.[8] It is within this atmosphere of rugged individualism and commercialization that adolescents struggle to come to maturity. Strong cultural narratives, which communicate that self-discovery is a solo and competitive pursuit and favor the individual and individualism at the expense of the communal, sideline relationships as ancillary or even at the expense of the good of the self and its self-promotion.

Amid the Sea of Humanity

Accompanying these narratives of independence and the structures of isolation is the dramatic growth in human population. Changes over the past century contribute to the challenges of forming and maintaining relationships today. For example, the sheer *volume* of connections and relationships we experience, the *mobility* and *speed* by which these connections form and interactions occur, and the tremendous *plurality* represented within those relationships. They collectively contribute to the challenge of recognizing, growing, and maintaining robust relationships, and the ability of adolescents and young adults to interpret their place in the world.

VOLUME

One of the facts of life in the twenty-first century is that we encounter—through multiple means—lots of people. While that may seem obvious, it is worthy of consideration for its impact on our ability to relate. As of this writing, the population of the United States is estimated at more than 325 million people. This means that it has *tripled* in the last century. While some of this is due to immigration, it is part of an overall global increase in population. As of 2017, the world population was estimated at more than seven billion.[9] This increase is due to many factors: advances in agriculture, food storage, and transportation have helped with food security;[10] health care has improved at both ends of the life cycle; more babies are born healthy and survive infancy; and people are living longer. The world's population from the beginning of human history increased very slowly, remaining under one billion people until the beginning of the Industrial Revolution, at which time it began to experience geometric growth. Then from 1959 to 1999—a mere forty-year period—the world population doubled, from three billion people to six billion people.[11]

For the sake of contrast, note that the five largest cities in Europe in the late Middle Ages topped out at 100,000. At that time, London held only sixty thousand people; today London has over 8.6 million people.[12] In 2014, the United States had ten cities with at least one million residents, with New York City topping the list at over 8.5 million people.[13] While we do not all live in such large cities, most of us live in urban settings, for there has also been a shift in where people live. Most United States' residents live in urban and suburban settings (75.2 percent in 1990), whereas the population a century earlier was primarily rural (60.4 percent in 1900).[14] Put simply, many of us physically encounter dramatically more people on a daily or weekly basis than a resident of medieval London would have met in his or her entire life. For a more recent contrast, it is likely that an adolescent growing up in the early twenty-first century will certainly encounter more people in his lifetime than an adolescent of the mid-twentieth century in the United States would have.

Communication technology researchers Lee Rainie and Barry Wellman argue that the triple revolution of new social networks, the internet, and mobile technologies have dramatically expanded the number and diversity of connections one person can have.[15] If we reflect on the number of people we encounter—whether face-to-face or electronically mediated—it can be dizzying or exhausting. Living in a dramatically expanded human community impacts our lives in terms of environmental sustainability, but the sheer volume makes its demands and takes its toll on our *social* sustainability—our ability to relate to one another in long-term, healthy ways. Humans have proven to be highly adaptable animals, but we are still social beings. We need to engage with one another, not only for day-to-day survival but also for our sense of place and value. An expanded human population raises existential questions: Do I need to be known by everyone to be known at all? Am I just a face in the crowd or do I matter to anyone? To which social group am I responsible? And who is responsible for me? Are they all? Do I only have to care for and about those I know? Or must I care for everyone? How can I?

The demands of living with many people are met in our daily communications and encounters. In school, work settings, teams, commuting, and shopping we meet in unmediated ways tens, hundreds, and even thousands of people a day, most of whom we do not know personally. Through the mediated forms—email, phone calls, texts, gaming, television, radio, social media outlets, and our favorite media feeds—we open ourselves up, and are opened to the lives of multiple, unseen others. Rainie and Wellman refer to this as our "social operating system," wherein each person is responsible for attending to and drawing on connections to meet needs and accomplish tasks.[16] Each of those connections—mediated and unmediated—makes demands on us. They call for our presence and attention, our concern, and maybe our action. In this way, we build social capital in relationships. For Putnam, "social capital refers to connections among individuals— social networks and the norms of reciprocity and trustworthiness that arise from them."[17] We develop social capital by investing in relationships, which we can then draw on as needed.[18] Even if we believe our ability to attend well to diverse stimuli is unlimited, our time is not.

Attempting to attend to so many connections makes it difficult to care well and deeply for any one of them. By being spread so widely, we are spread thinly. The volume of people with whom we interact undermines our ability to develop relationships deeply.

MOBILITY AND SPEED

The mobility and speed of our lives add to the stress felt by the volume of connections. By the early twenty-first century, we have become accustomed to mobility, but the frequency and distance of our moves is a relatively recent phenomenon. Many of us—as families or individuals—change residential communities multiple times in our lives. Sometimes the move is within the same metropolitan area, but those areas can be quite large. Other times, it is across the country or the globe. Consider also that most extended families live at a distance from one another, but we expect to keep connected. Moves do not necessarily mean—as they once did—that we sever relationships with those who are no longer close at hand. New forms of communication and the ease of long-distance travel allow us to continue the relationships—or even residences—in more than one location. This frequent movement undermines the investments of time and energy in any community. Putnam claims that the demands of "suburbanization, commuting, and sprawl" contribute to a decline in civic engagement.[19] In each of these cases, we simply add to the volume and the expectation of connection and attention. Yet those of us who have attempted to maintain multiple locations or relationships over a distance know such work can undermine—or simply discourage—investing deeply in new relationships in the new setting.

Even if they and their family have not moved, young people experience frequent changes in classmates, teachers, coaches, and all manner of others. It is also increasingly common that, from an early age (preteen), adolescents are participating in extracurricular activities that require regular travel and engagement within nonoverlapping communities (for example, traveling soccer teams, church-sponsored youth groups, Irish step dancing).[20] Participation in multiple communities of engagement persists for them through young adulthood, when many take on diverse activity groupings through their college years. Consider also the hours in a week or a month that are spent traveling among these various communities. The mobility among these nonoverlapping communities almost necessarily increases the speed with which we interact with any one of the communities or their members. Frequently, the "free time" for exchanges between an adult and an adolescent happens during the commute or on the sidelines of the activities, but that same free time may also be spent digitally "tethered" to those who are not there rather than with those physically present.[21] This is not to disparage the value of these diverse activities or communities.[22] Note the variety of settings and volume of people in a contemporary young person's life. Being present among so many communities and in rapid succession undermines our ability to know and be known well by any one of them.

PLURALITY

Finally, each community, relationship, or network of relationships makes demands—has expectations. To repeat the language of the prior chapter, each relationship or network provides a context needing interpretation. And each one may be subtly or dramatically different from another. Ask any student in school if all teachers and classrooms are alike and the response likely will be a hearty, "No!" Even in a relatively cohesive setting, like a school, expectations and demands vary. Similarly, within a family there may be diverse expectations, especially if that family is at odds with itself. Extrapolate these relatively cohesive environments to the multiple relationships and communities an adolescent or young adult has and you begin to appreciate the plurality of expectations and demands with which they live.

That plurality is compounded by the diversity of the United States. There are regional variations as different ethnic, cultural, economic, racial, and religious communities have settled and developed various locations and have had different histories in those locations. What is valued and celebrated in Texas may not have the same sway in Oregon and vice versa. As our mobility has us shift social settings, we encounter and need to learn these differences. Also, over the past half century, the United States has come to be the most religiously plural country in the world. This was initiated with the changes in immigration laws in the 1960s that eased quotas on non-European immigrants. Since then, people from all over the world, not just Europe, have come to make the United States their home, bringing with them their religious, ethnic, and cultural lives.[23] Practices valued in

24

Mumbai, India, may not be recognized as such in Minneapolis; but, at the same time, the cultural practices in Minneapolis are shaped by those brought from Mumbai. For many young people, they encounter this diversity in school, from elementary to postsecondary. But they also encounter it in their neighborhoods and even families. Each of the people they encounter has hopes and expectations, which may be similar in their grand scheme, but differ sufficiently in their particulars to be confusing. The diversity itself is not necessarily problematic. However, making sense amid diversity is more challenging than learning the expectations of a homogenous world. There is so much more to learn in the face of such diversity and a greater need to develop capacities for interpretation and discernment.

Adolescence Experienced Differently

These larger cultural realities frame the experience of adolescents and families and contribute to the structures of isolation that are now prevalent. Structural isolation refers to those habits and patterns of daily life that make it difficult to establish and foster relationships with select important people, both inside and outside of immediate families, while simultaneously managing hundreds or thousands of contacts and connections. Current social structures have served to isolate adolescents into age peer groupings and away from adults. And they have also served to isolate immediate households from one another, thus burdening the parent with the role of sole adult model and support for their adolescent children. The separation of adolescents from adults (and families from one another) makes it difficult for the development of enduring and robust relationships between adolescents and adults who are not their parents. Beyond the population changes noted earlier, there are several interrelated factors that contribute to structural isolation of adolescents, some of which have been developing over centuries so that their impact has gone largely unnoticed.

Structural isolation of adolescents has not always been the case, and perhaps need not be in the future. In a previous article, I argued that "for most of human history young people have grown to adulthood within small, intergenerational, and relatively stable communities of people, all of which would have contributed to the opportunity to make meaningful relationships with adults in their midst."[24] If we look to premodern Europe, the historically dominant cultural influence of the United States, we can appreciate how the changes over the past several centuries have shaped where we are today. Prior to the technological explosion of the Industrial Revolution of the eighteenth century, most people were born, came to maturity, and died within geographically and socially stable communities, wherein populations were small and travel was limited. Enduring relationships among children, adolescents, and adults of all ages would have been relatively easy, simply because there were fewer people to know and few opportunities to meet new people. I am not suggesting that the relationships themselves were easy, nor am I romanticizing premodern people or periods. It is important to note the difference in social worlds, in terms of small numbers and stability in populations within a given locale. Such stable and small communities of people would have been the experience of most humans prior to the modern age, and thus the relational setting in which adolescents came to maturity. Adolescents would have spent their days and years surrounded by people of all ages whom they knew well and who knew them. This would have provided the opportunity to have significant relationships with multiple adults beyond their parents, simply by the fact of opportunity.[25] Among those adults who knew them, some would have invested in them and challenged the youth to invest in the community. However, changes in labor and transportation over the past few centuries have dramatically impacted how children, adolescents, and adults spend their days, such that these groups have become largely segregated from one another. Unlike centuries ago, today, there is not the same deep familiarity among adolescents and adults who are not their parents.

For much of human history, adults worked near to where they lived, very often in the same building. If they were agricultural laborers, which most were, they lived close to the land they cultivated. As early as children were able, they took on tasks relative to home and labor, growing in skill and responsibility over time. If adolescent or older children went into service or apprenticeships, they lived in the homes of those to whom they were contracted, usually for years at a time. Thus, over time, they came to maturity within the ongoing presence of multiple adults and learned vocational skills in their company. It would have been rare for them to spend time with large numbers of their age peers.[26] The removal of adult work from the home progressed throughout the eighteenth and nineteenth centuries with the development of industrialization. The colonization and development of North America reflects the later stages of that progression, shifting from small, rural agriculture and small-scale manufacturing toward urbanization and industrialization. Finally, the removal of children and young adolescents from most workplaces and the introduction of compulsory education were accomplished in the early twentieth century. Each of these changes contributed to where, how, and with whom children and adolescents spent their day. As adults no longer worked at home, children needed to be cared for elsewhere. As work and work environments became more technically complicated, preparation for work was elongated and mandatory schooling extended through adolescence.

Today, when adults are at work, children and adolescents are in school or other activities, preparing for eventual work. The same economy of scale that informed and shaped modern labor (e.g., efficiency, repeatability, and uniformity) likewise shaped modern education, whereby schools became larger, more standardized, and segregated into age peer grouping to serve larger populations more efficiently, professionally, and economically. There are adults involved in these other settings, but the adults' interactions are in accord with their roles in those settings (e.g., teacher, administrator, therapist, coach, or tutor) and not as their full adult selves living their day-to-day lives. In those settings, there are frequently high ratios of adolescents to adults, requiring the adult to manage discrete interactions with multiple young people. Additionally, those relationships between specific adults and youth (e.g., one teacher to a classroom of students) change on a regular basis, whether annually or more frequently. In the school setting, the most enduring relationships are usually among large numbers of age peers, many of whom will be in school together for years. Simply, the changes experienced in labor since the dawn of the Industrial Revolution have dramatically altered where, and in whose company, adolescents come to maturity. Whereas adolescents used to live within intergenerational settings that allowed for stable relationships that endured over the course of years, by the mid-twentieth century, for the first time in human history, most adolescents are in large age peer groupings with limited opportunities for ongoing relationships with anyone outside that grouping, particularly adults who are not their parents. This segregation practice has impacted the opportunity for adolescents and nonparent adults to form enduring relationships. It has also hindered adolescents' ability to properly understand adult lives and imagine themselves as adults.

Building on the concerns of mobility previously discussed, similar patterns of movement can be found in the daily schedules of contemporary adolescents, who divide time among school, jobs, activities, and sports, many of which require commuting. Very often, each move is between distinct organizations with separate, nonoverlapping memberships. This movement affects different populations in diverse ways, with some depending more on public transportation and others on private. Regardless, constant movement across communities allows for diverse opportunities and encounters for adolescents in a day or a week, but it also limits opportunities for adolescents to know and be known well within each community such that they are both beneficiaries and contributors. As such, it can limit their ability to develop social capital.

Being at Home in the Sea of Humanity

Rainie and Wellman's concept of "networked individualism" is helpful in articulating this twenty-first-century reality. It acknowledges that today's adolescent is not living within a tightly bounded and cohesive community, nor is he an island, unconnected and unresponsive to others. Rather, he lives within networks connecting him with others across diverse and distant contexts.[27] Within his network, he has a few close ties, usually to family; many more "weak ties" with friends, friends of friends; and countless latent ties, waiting to be brought to life.[28] While they have been able to describe his networked connections, Rainie and Wellman have not been able to articulate how he learns the skills of relating—particularly of developing robust relationships from "latent" and "weak links" and connections—except to say that "larger networks provide more social support" simply because they have the higher potential to connect the individual to needed assets.[29] But they also warn that most "individuals have 'sparsely knit' personal communities, meaning that most network members are not directly connected with one another;" each connection is specialized for certain tasks, and they do not communicate among themselves.[30] There are challenges inherent in this social model. First, the adolescent must recognize and advocate for his needs himself. For example, he may feel lonely and overwhelmed, but afraid to tell anyone else for fear they will judge him harshly. Second, the network may remain ignorant of problems if he chooses not to share, or unable to help if unconnected to or unaware of other links in the network.

Conclusion

In this brief review of social change, it is important to note that there is no single culprit, but many dynamics that have evolved over time to contribute to structures that serve to isolate adolescents from the company of adults beyond their parents. Humans have been passing through adolescence toward adulthood as long as there have been people old enough to do so. It is not unique to our time. However, the current structures of isolation and the cultural messages of individualism and consumption are unique to this era. All are detrimental to meeting the various relational and interpretive tasks of adolescence in a healthy way. The cultural narratives of individualism and consumption offer a lonely horizon upon which a person might imagine his life. Likewise, the structures of isolation amid the sea of humanity offer countless people with whom he might interact but make it hard for him to find and grow trustworthy companions, especially mature adults, with whom he might reflect and imagine. The most troubling is that amid a sea of humanity, it is difficult for him to find someone who will recognize him as a unique and valuable person. The conditions make it challenging for him to establish relationships where he is convincingly affirmed for who he is. And he finds it difficult to do likewise for another. Instead, he feels like he is casting about alone upon the waves, grabbing at flotsam and jetsam, despairing of finding safe harbor.

3

Relying on Instruments

One allure of sailing is simply being amid the elements of water, wind, and weather. Sailing calls for an evergrowing practice of watchfulness that draws the sailor into the moment. In recent years, it has become common to sail with electronic instruments. They are especially helpful on long trips in unfamiliar waters. Electronic charts and course plotters help plan your trip; depth and wind monitors keep track of current conditions. While good and helpful tools, the temptation is to draw the sailor's focus to the monitors and away from the conditions on the water. Rather than augment her attentiveness, they replace it, changing the experience and opening opportunities for accidents. Furthermore, the novice sailor, by relying heavily on instrumentation, may never gain the skills of reading the wind and the current. Similarly, with the availability of digital and increasingly mobile technology, we can be drawn to the technology and away from the experience of the relationship they are intended to aid.

Amid this volume, speed, mobility, and plurality discussed in the previous chapter, it is easy to meet multiple fascinating people and to revel in the world of possibilities. However, it is difficult to be known and know others well, if for no other reason than the limitations of time. In that regard, digital technology should be a help, in that it allows for speedy communication with many people, even those at a great distance. But does it always help? There is certainly a place for technological communication, and unquestionably an allure to it, but the opportunities it offers are not always aids. Here we identify briefly some of the specific challenges to technologically mediated communications, how they shape our relational practices, and how they may affect the ways we learn to relate and develop robust relationships.

Practicing Digitally Mediated Connections

For adolescents and young adults in the early twenty-first century, digital communication has been a part of their lives from an early age and is increasingly the mode of interaction throughout their day. In 2015, the Pew Research Center published a report of a study in which they investigated the use of technology by teens (ages thirteen to seventeen), analyzing it across racial and social economic lines. The study found that 92 percent of these teens go online daily; of these as many as 56 percent go online multiple times a day, with African American and Hispanic youth logging the most frequent internet use.[1] Besides race, the research discovered that household income factors into whether youth have access at home to desktops or laptops, with wealthier households the most likely to have one or both. As a result, white teens have greater access to desktop and laptop computers. However, the same report found that "African-American teens are the most likely of any group of teens to have a smartphone, with 85% having access to one, compared with 71% of both White and Hispanic teens."[2] The report indicates that teen access and use of digital technology cuts across racial and socioeconomic lines.

Whether this access is good or bad is debated among various voices.[3] In this section, we rely on technology researchers danah boyd, Sherry Turkle, Lee Rainie, and Barry Wellman, each of whom offers a balanced assessment of technology use. An important starting point is offered by boyd, who argues that teens are not obsessed with the technology; they are obsessed with connecting and fitting in with their peers. This is a valuable point in that it is, she claims, the same task that adolescents have been doing for generations, even though the platforms have changed over time.[4] Rainie and Wellman make a similar claim, writing that "people are not hooked on gadgets—they are hooked on each other."[5] While Turkle does not challenge these points, in recent writing she has moved from an earlier, more optimistic stance concerning technology to a stance wherein she is worried about the impact of technology on the quality of human interactions.[6] Turkle notes the multiple ways in which technology is used to retreat from direct engagement so as to limit emotional availability and vulnerability.[7]

While neither Turkle nor boyd comment on the volume of connections, the retreat from direct engagement is—in part—an effort to manage the sheer volume of encounters and connections in our lives and make up for the fact that we have limited face-to-face time with most of these connections. The technologies allow us to connect to more people by sharing more widely (social media, online forums, blogs, feeds) or more expediently with individuals (texts, messaging, emails). However, while it helps us manage the current volume of connections, it also encourages an expansion of that volume; it takes little effort to include one more recipient on an email, add one more "friend," or "follow" someone new. Yet each adds expectations—whether mailing, following, or posting—of time, attention, and interest. So while digital technologies help manage the volume of connections, they easily add to that volume, which then calls for greater monitoring of those digital spaces. And as the popular platforms change, which is especially the case among adolescents who are looking to be on the same platforms as their peers, monitoring more digital spaces is required. All this managing and monitoring can be a source of anxiety, but more immediately their use draws us into practices with the technology that are not in service to relationships.

"I ♥ MY...!"

As noted earlier, boyd argues, "Most teens are not compelled by gadgetry as such—they are compelled by friendship. The gadgets are interesting to them primarily as a means to a social end."[8] It allows them to connect with peers with whom they have limited, unstructured, unmonitored, face-to-face time.[9] However, the technology does not necessarily accomplish relational goals. The first issue is our relationship with the technology itself. It is a love-hate relationship where we love the technology for how and with whom it can connect us; we keep up with people's news even if we are not able to spend time with them face-to-face. But we hate it when it fails to work as we hope and when it pulls us in too many directions; when it pulls us away from the present, and when we are ignored by others who are so pulled.

Devices themselves become the "portal" through which relationships are experienced. For some, the separation from the device is felt as separation from companionship.[10] This is increasingly true as we turn to more mobile technologies. Because they live in our pockets or strapped to our wrists, we never leave behind potential connections. The relationship with the device becomes immediate; the people become mediated. As the devices allow for constant "tethering" to the lives of those not physically present, Turkle writes, we are rendered "absent" to the immediate.[11] Even if a device sits on a table, it represents potential interruptions. It pings, rings, vibrates, or glows and attention is taken from the immediate in favor of the mediated.[12]

Furthermore, the mediated formats tend to flatten the difference in importance among our relationships. While boyd found that "most teens use a plethora of social media services as they navigate relationships and contexts" addressing distinct audiences on each platform, I would still argue that the modes shape the communication.[13] Texts and messaging—used for more private communications—tend to abbreviate interchanges. Whereas more public fora (social media, blogs, and feeds) offer longer communiqués by a scattershot means of broadcasting. Rainie and Wellman note that Facebook profiles, for example, "are set up to default to the assumption that all people want to make all their information available to all of their Facebook friends."[14] Frequently, important relations receive the same information—and in the same format—as those less intimate. This is not to suggest we do not have some affection for all our connections, but the constant use of these media blurs the distinctions among them.

Finally, if we spend most of our time in mediated relations, we advantage that format and disadvantage the skills of face-to-face relating.[15] Simply, we become good at what we practice. We can easily become unreflective users, allowing the technology and other people's expectations for it to drive how it is used. We can lose sight of our relational objectives. That which is designed to keep us connected becomes a means of disconnection from or partial attention to what is important to us. We need to be mindful of how we differentiate among the tens, hundreds, or thousands of connections such that we nurture, and are nurtured, by those few that are most important. Rather than simply avoid mediated forms of relating, we may have to develop practices around their use that help and do not undermine the relationships they are designed to serve.

LOOKING FOR CONTROL—
AVOIDING VULNERABILITY

We, by our Pavlovian response to the rings, pings, and vibrations, intimate that we welcome the intrusion. However, Turkle observes an increased aversion to the immediacy of live phone conversations.[16] She notices a shift toward preferring texts, messaging, and other forms that create space in the interaction, such that we can keep our emotional responses at a distance from the immediate exchange. The mediated space in some ways promises greater control than the face-to-face encounter. Through texts or posts we can be selective about what we disclose; our face is not available to give away our feelings; we can react to others invisibly. The technology creates a buffer. Turkle describes adolescent girls' avoidance: "These young women prefer to deal with strong feelings from the safe haven of the Net. It gives them an alternative to processing emotions in real time. Under stress, they seek composure above all. But they do not find equanimity."[17] Turkle repeatedly found that adolescents especially used mediated forms to sidestep the immediacy and vulnerability of emotions. They claim that "texting offers protection."[18] However, the protection may be an illusion, for it creates a new pressure of appearing constantly composed.

In these efforts, we can discern two related desires: one is to present oneself flawlessly; the other is to respond flawlessly. Yet this desire for control is illusory. Boyd argues, "These digital bodies are fundamentally coarser, making it far easier to misinterpret what someone is expressing."[19] While the young author may be selective in what he has shared, he is not able to see how it is interpreted. So he cannot respond immediately with corrections or explanations. Even if the exchange is in almost real time—like texting or messaging—the physical absence of the reader allows for the possibility of the intended reader to invite an unseen third—or more—into the "private" exchange.[20] Unintended readers can read and offer their anonymous reactions to the original posting before the originator has a chance to correct or clarify the intention.[21]

The technology allows a too-easy escape from the awkwardness or time consumption of face-to-face or real-time encounters. While initially attractive, such avoidance means we never overcome the awkwardness or become less self-conscious in the engagement. What seems like avoidance is only postponement; we are all awkward until we are surer of ourselves. We learn the skills of conversation in their exercise, especially in intimate settings like those among close friends and family.[22] If we limit face-to-face conversations to lighthearted or brief exchanges, the subtle and careful skills of conversation in more trying, loaded, or difficult moments remain a mystery, not only for those intimate settings but also for public engagement.[23] Finally, by avoiding the face-to-face interaction, we miss potential moments of affection and grace that come with such encounters. Again, we get good at what we practice and never get good at what we do not practice.

INVISIBLE AUDIENCE—TO WHOM AM I RESPONSIBLE?

In part, the desire to present a flawless image comes from not really knowing at any given moment to whom you are communicating and the context of that communication's reception. Most adolescents—and even mature adults—imagine they know the audiences of their mediated communications even though readers and the settings in which they are reading are invisible. Adolescents and young adults usually share texts, messaging, and social media with people they know face-to-face. However, those are readable and available to countless others. Nevertheless, adolescents and young adults compose blogs, personal web pages, and feeds as a means of identity exploration and expression, and to find audiences beyond the people they know face-to-face. Technology researcher Susannah Stern reports that creators usually identify themselves as their primary audience; similar to anyone who has ever kept a journal or diary, they are writing themselves into self-reflection.[24] Secondarily, creators seek validation from invisible audiences. Even if they are displayed in public sites available to unknown others, adolescents perceive their postings as private communications that should not be read by those the author hopes to exclude.[25]

While this clearly raises concern for security, it also raises questions of responsibility. Responsibility is learned within the context of relationships; relational settings foster the development of care and concern as well as communicate the particulars of acceptable and unacceptable behavior. However, invisible audiences are easier to dismiss. Stern's research indicates a tendency among teen authors to dismiss the critical comments of responders whose value is not already established with the teen.[26] Similarly, Turkle notes that when we encounter people who do not interest us, or with whom we disagree, there is a dispatch with which we treat them such that "we invent ways of being with people that turn them into something close to things."[27] Such dismissal is evident in cyberbullying; because the victim is invisible, the young person cannot easily imagine the hurt caused by the bullying, but he can imagine the consequences to himself of nonparticipation. His life is real; the unseen victim is less so.[28]

Developing a sense of responsibility relates to developing a sense of care for others. Care and responsibility reflect a person's capacity to move beyond immediate self-interest to see and learn to attend to the needs of another. Rainie and Wellman refer to these relational invest-ments and exchanges as "social capital." An individual needs social capital so he can draw upon it in moments of need.[29] However, to do so, he needs to come to know the other—who they are, what they feel, what is important to them—in order to respond appropriately. Fur-thermore, he develops emotional intelligence—how to read the sub-tlety of emotions—over time in face-to-face encounters.[30] When the other remains invisible and anonymous, these opportunities are miss-ing. Rather, the individual is encouraged to reflect only on himself—how he is perceived and validated—as the only known player in the exchange. Ongoing engagement with invisible audiences lacks the prompts for care and responsibility beyond his concerns and encour-ages self-consciousness but not necessarily self-awareness.

ARE YOU THERE? / ARE YOU REAL?

However, the invisible audience is not only consequential for how we respond to them, but for what they offer us. The invisible audience lacks context. We do not know from where they speak, if they are real or fictitious, or if their responses to us are authentic. Both Stern and boyd write of how important online affirmations are to young authors. Boyd writes that they are "part of the more general desire to be validated by one's peers."[31] But how are they to know whether the affirmations or critiques are authentic? Similarly, Turkle finds that users frequently invest in personalities they discover online (e.g., avatars, blogs) while simultaneously wondering how real they are.[32] Playing to the invis-ible audience while being unsure of the same audience's validity puts us in a double bind. We work for the validation while questioning its real value, but we are too scared to move in a new direction and risk losing what we have. We present who we believe others want us to be while remaining unsure of whether there is real affirmation for what we present.

Avatars, profiles, blogs, feeds, and websites offer valuable space for expression and experimentation. But the feedback remains questionable without confirmation in an eventual face-to-face encounter, when the anonymity ends. Humans need the love and concern of others; we need affirmation and connection.

AM I REAL?

Conversely, we need to ask if our representations are fully authentic. Boyd celebrates digital sites as spaces where adolescents can explore their sense of self without the consequence of immediate reactions. Websites, social media, and blogs allow adolescents "more control online—they can choose what information to put forward, thereby eliminating visceral reactions that might have seeped out in everyday communication."[33] Similarly, Turkle notes that the mediated formats invite a certain performance, in that one chooses what is made public.[34] Rainie and Wellman note that "people have more freedom to tailor their interactions."[35] These modes allow for editing one's real life so that they may appear more attractive to audiences. The technology also allows for designing a persona for distinct audiences; those audiences can then remain separate and ignorant of different, conflicting persona.[36] We omit what we think will not appeal or will be rejected by a quick swipe of an app. Or we shape ourselves into what we believe people want. We can try things out in ways we never would in front of people we know. This can be liberating, especially if we are unsure of acceptance among our immediate community.

Granted, as a young adolescent begins to become self-conscious of being seen by others, it is natural to try on different poses or personas to see how they feel and how others respond. Thus the possibility of limited and selective exposure and the absence of consequences are initially attractive. But if the bridge to the face-to-face world is not made, its absence can contribute to further isolation as she lives a fractured life. The value of that acceptance is not felt in the interactions with the people known in real life. Similarly, she may be compelled to present a perfect "princess" image of herself to attract the perfect "prince," in hope of the perfect long-term relationship. When that prince turns out

37

to be another warty toad, who also threatens to expose her warts, she tosses him and frantically scans the pond in hopes of finding the true ready-made prince. Thus the cycle of image control and surveillance continues endlessly, and it certainly does not advance toward the goal of her being discovered and valued for her personhood.

DISTRACTED FROM MYSELF

The siren song of technology is that we will find connection to the wider world—people, ideas, and possibilities. However, it also draws our attention away from investigating our own impressions, ideas, desires, and vulnerable self-reflection. Turkle and boyd both write of users being constantly drawn to their devices as a means of keeping current with their worlds. However, the same devices that connect us with others can be a means of escaping from a deep encounter with ourselves. Presented with free time and the threat of facing our own thoughts, we reach for our devices to read feeds, watch videos, listen to music (perhaps all at once), or record our own words for distribution on our texts, tweets, or blogs. The smartphone in hand feeds into and encourages our "FOMO" (fear of missing out). Our constant consumption of more public material offers a way to avoid engaging with our private selves. Referring to the capacity for mobile technology to "accelerate" our efforts to connect outside ourselves, Turkle writes, "Rapid cycling stabilizes into a sense of copresence. Even a simple cell phone brings us into the world of continual partial attention."[37] This continual partial attention keeps us from going deeply into any single task or idea. Instead, like a water bug remaining buoyant on the surface by spreading its weight across six separate points, we skim over the top, afraid of being drawn in deeply at any single point.

It takes the adolescent—and the adult—time and solitude to become aware of, and then comfortable with, his thoughts, feelings, and desires. It takes even more time for him to discern how each may change over time and due to circumstance, to learn what endures and what is passing. By avoiding—and so remaining on the surface—of his inner world, he is more likely to remain self-conscious and not move to the deeper work of self-awareness. Self-consciousness can entrap him in focusing on others' reaction to him, what they think and like about him. The focus on their reactions can keep him from seeing what he understands and likes about himself, to come to identify what is true and enduring in him.[38]

Promise versus Delivery

Opting out of using digital communication is not possible in the twenty-first century. It is used in nearly every aspect of our lives. While it may not be a substitution, "people will make do with electronic contact if they cannot be together in person."[39] However, Rainie and Wellman find that users "have to work harder to figure out which gadget or mobile apps to use for which kind of activity." For while "the internet is especially good for connecting people with their weaker ties and with a broader diversity of people" and allows for an extension of our social networks, it requires considerable time and effort on the part of the individual to maintain those ties and connections.[40]

For today's adolescents and young adults, it is increasingly the case that relationships are initiated and maintained primarily or exclusively through digital means, thus shaping the imaginative norm by which the relationship is experienced.[41] However, this has its pitfalls alongside its possibilities. In many ways, the technological platforms undermine the incremental process of developing the skills of relating: learning to be vulnerable; learning to be trustworthy; learning to get over awkwardness and self-consciousness; seeing how we impact others and how they impact us; developing an integrated identity. These are not all-or-nothing abilities or a matter of being perfect. We learn these skills incrementally; first awkwardly, and then with time and practice we gain refinement, but never with a guarantee of perfection. The back-and-forth movements of affection, risk, vulnerability, hurt, reconciliation, renewed affection, and increased trust take time and space. They are developed within the context of real people who confront us by their realness and do not let us turn away but encourage us with love and care to work through the difficulty to find the joy.[42] This back and forth is exactly what contributes to relationships becoming robust and intimate. To avoid the risks altogether is to avoid the prospect of knowing and being known.

While valuable for managing volume and diversity of connections, especially weak ties, digital technology may not be the best aid for learning and developing robust relationships and the skills of relating. Thus we need to develop practices for using the technology that limits it to what it does well. Without some reflection, our practices around the use of digital media can make our relating more problematic instead of better. The rise and pervasiveness of digital technologies raises the stakes for our need to be very intentional about communicating and practicing the skills of relating well, for the digital settings by their nature largely undermine those skills.

Missing Opportunities for Grace

Although I have named some challenges to robust relationships in the twenty-first century, is there anything really at stake? Is it possible that in the pursuit of the many connections or the perfect partner, we miss the opportunity for grace that is found in the relationship that is right in front of us? To make sense of this, let's turn again to theologian Karl Rahner, who articulated a conception of grace that spoke to God's ever-present reality as well as human freedom. Rahner, drawing from scholastic theology, distinguished between *created* and *uncreated* grace. Edward Hahnenberg, interpreting Rahner, writes, "*Uncreated grace* referred to God Godself, the indwelling of the Trinity in the human soul." Whereas *created grace* "referred to a gratuitous gift from God, which was distinct from God, that led to a positive change in the human person."[43] Rahner argued that uncreated grace always precedes created grace. The human person does not make herself acceptable to God prior to receiving God's created grace; God is already present and active as uncreated grace. Hahnenberg writes, "God becomes present to us in love, and that love prompts the change within us." Furthermore, "grace is not primarily an external reality pushing people from outside; it is an inner constitutive principle of the human person."[44] God's gracious self-communication precedes the human person's perception of it, and, Rahner argues, "hence the acceptance of grace is once again an event of grace itself."[45] Therefore, as the person opens herself to grace (uncreated), more grace (created) ensues. Grace builds on grace.

If we understand that relationships can serve as a means of experiencing and perceiving God's grace through love experienced with another, then the quality of relationships becomes important. For an experience of self-giving love felt in a relationship is an experience of God's self-gift, even while God is not limited by that relationship. But self-giving love is seldom expressed or discovered on the fly. Rather, it takes time and attention, usually vulnerability and trust, to be felt, recognized, acknowledged, and reciprocated. It involves an appreciation of one another's personhood. As the adolescent opens himself to another person and is recognized as a unique person in mutual self-giving, his opportunity to receive grace increases. Again, grace builds on grace. Such an experience of love is not likely perceived with every connection and encounter. However, the experience of it in some of his relationships encourages him to look for it in any relationship. He becomes attuned to discovering and giving love in any encounter. However, if he skims across the surface of multiple connections, he misses an opportunity for grace experienced in the depths of specific relationships.

Skimming over the surface impairs the recognition of grace in the immediate and concrete experience of another, but skimming also impairs his ability to sense the infinite underneath the surface of life, what Rahner describes as an *unthematic* experience of God. A *thematic experience* of God is an idea or conception about God; it is an effort to bring to articulation the *unthematic*, the unknowable, inarticulate experience that grounds all experience.[46] Rahner writes, "In the ultimate depths of his being man knows nothing more surely than that his knowledge...is only a small island in a vast sea that has not been traveled. It is a floating island, and it might be more familiar to us than the sea, but ultimately it is borne by the sea and only because it is can we be borne by it."[47] As I referenced in chapter 1, Rahner warns that "if a person wants...he can always choose to accept this infinite question only as a thorn in the side of his knowledge" and not open himself up to the infinite.[48] His countless human connections are many of the floating islands that can attract all his attention and distract him from the larger question *that* there are islands—their source, purpose, and end—and something greater and other supports them and makes them possible. The adolescent, newly able to see himself as distinct from his world, stands at the threshold of such questions. Like the novice sailor who learns to look beyond the boat, these larger questions can best be acknowledged if he stops to lift his attention from the immediate and allows himself to pay attention long enough to encounter the transcendent that has been there all along.

Finally, reception of grace and recognition of himself on the horizon of the transcendent is an act of freedom for the adolescent. Freedom, as argued by Rahner, is "not the power to be able to do this or that, but the power to decide about oneself and to actualize oneself."[49] This freedom determines what we will call "little" freedoms, such as the freedom from compulsions that keep him distracted from himself and from the transcendent; or the freedom from conforming to some external norm of acceptability. Yet the greater freedom that Rahner names is a freedom *for*; it is the freedom "that he accepts his own self as it is disclosed and offered to him."[50] In chapter 4, we draw on Catherine LaCugna, who builds on Rahner's concept of freedom *for*, by marrying it to John Zizioulas's concept of ecstatic personhood. By doing so, she reminds us that this self the adolescent receives is not for himself alone. She writes, "The actualization of personhood takes place in self-transcendence, the movement of freedom toward communion with other persons."[51] Freedom allows him, through the grace of God, to move beyond his own limited concerns and boundaries to be present for and with the other. Bringing these lines of thought together, we can say that the most profound and fundamental freedom for the adolescent—as for all persons—is the freedom to accept himself as a gift of God, and to give himself as gift to another.

Conclusion

The discovery and reception of the adolescent as a person of unique value is accomplished in and through robust relationships that recognize her, draw her forth, and celebrate her. The challenge of the number, speed, mobility, and mediated nature of her connections is that in pursuit of thousands of potential relationships, she is never known well enough in any one of them. In pursuit of countless "likes," she can miss the opportunity to build self-giving love with another. Amid the endless possible connections, she searches for the perfect ready-made relationship and never learns that relationships are grown, not delivered. She is like the sailor who over-relies on instruments to understand the sailing conditions and misses the experience of sailing.

Relying on Instruments

Just as the novice sailor needs the guidance of more seasoned sailors to show her how to read the wind and the water, an adolescent needs trustworthy adults to help her interpret relationships and suggest reliable courses. Just as the novice sailor needs to see that the wind and waves as not frightening hazards, but full of grace and opportunity, so too the adolescent needs to learn that real relationships require trust, vulnerability, responsibility, and forgiveness. While each may seem frightening, they are essential for love to grow. For the adolescent, robust relationships can become the locations for discerning God's grace. In them, adolescents and adults can share the practices of watchfulness and attention, reading and making sense of the stormy conditions so that God's grace might be discovered amid it all.

Part Two

INTO DEEPER
WATERS

Every child literally outgrows the *Optimist*—the boat they first learn to sail; they become too large and heavy to sail it safely. To keep sailing, the young sailor has to move onto larger boats. Larger boats allow our sailor to travel farther and in greater safety; however, they require more people, more sails, and deeper water. The move to larger boats brings new challenges, particularly those of understanding a more complicated boat, working with other people, and reading the conditions, especially in new settings. In this part of the book, we discuss how the expectations of adulthood come unbidden, just like the need to move out of *Opti*, and demand the adolescent respond. They can no longer depend on others to make decisions for them but must learn to do so themselves. They can no longer stay in the safe waters close to shore, for life will bring them out to deeper and unknown places.

Although we use the sailing metaphor, let us not become distracted with the need to set a destination, as if adulthood is a place one reaches like a distant harbor. Rather, pay attention to how we travel—how we interpret the conditions and work together. Adulthood, as argued in chapter 4, is a way of proceeding; it is *the capacity to be responsible within the context of relationships*. Therefore, adolescence is the time of first *learning* and *mastering* certain tasks: recognizing oneself as a person; recognizing the personhood of others; and recognizing and living into relationships. In chapter 5, we discuss how relationships and communities communicate values, identity, and purpose to the adolescent. Relationships provide a horizon upon which he interprets and imagines his life. Just as sailing requires attention to the setting—like wind, current, and other factors—it is incumbent on the adolescent to interpret his world.

4

Charting a Course

For the purposes of this book, it is most helpful to consider the transition from childhood to adulthood as a single, lengthy, and nuanced process of transformation from an *instrumental* engagement with the world—as is suitable and acceptable for childhood—toward a *relational* engagement. While it is commonly held that relationships and social worlds are a new concern for adolescents, I argue that the capacities to initiate, grow, and maintain relationships are central expectations of adult maturity, making good relationships essential for adolescent maturation. I support this claim theologically. For this, I rely on the theology of Catherine LaCugna: that we are made by God to relate; it is through our relationships that God reveals Godself to us and God reveals us to ourselves and to others; and we are called to live out our love of God in relationships of love with one another.

Adulthood in a Relational Perspective

Adulthood is a socially constructed reality; its externals vary with the expectations of the relationships and communities within which a person is located.[1] Yet frequently when defining adulthood, there is a tendency to refer only to external markers like acquiring a driver's license, buying alcohol legally, serving in the armed forces, or voting in an election.[2] But even a quick review of this short list reveals that there are different ages for each of these, fixed by state or federal authorities. Other markers—like full-time employment, getting married, or living

47

on one's own—also vary according to economic and social opportunity as well as cultural expectation.[3] Or we might also look to the age by which one is able to get pregnant or impregnate others, but here we see a biological definition that varies from individual to individual. Even among religious markers, there is variety. Jews reaching the age of thirteen can read the *Torah* publicly at religious services, but few synagogues would put full responsibility in the hands of a thirteen-year-old. As for Christians, confirmation is sometimes identified as a marker of adulthood, but the sacrament is celebrated at different ages in different denominations and dioceses. Still others may suggest that adulthood is when you "feel like an adult," but that presupposes a reasonable understanding of what adulthood should "feel like."[4] With so much disagreement among all these authoritative sources—state, federal, psychological, sociological, biological, and religious—any desire to determine a clear arrival or age by static external markers is quickly frustrated. However, when we consider internal capacities—like responsibility, consideration for others, and the ability to think and decide for oneself—there is more universal agreement that these qualities are essential for adulthood.[5]

Adulthood is best understood as successful interplay between internal capacities and external demands. Adulthood is the capacity to be *responsible within the context of relationships*, which demands an awareness of oneself, other people, situations, and of the consequence of one's action or inaction. In other words, it demands the ability to see and act in the world *relationally*. Mature adults demonstrate the ability to interplay between fluid, external expectations (rather than simple, external markers of achievement) and have the internal capacities to meet or negotiate those expectations, like negotiating conflicts between work and family life. Therefore, what responsibility within relationships looks like—how it gets enacted in concrete externals—remains open, as we will see later. For the moment, I emphasize that adult lives are strongly framed by the relationships within which they function and are not intelligently (or usefully) conceivable outside of or apart from the demands (and benefits) of those relationships. Recognizing and accounting for those relationships—their demands, costs, and benefits—is a central expectation of adults. Thus, *learning* to see and meet relational expectations is the single hardest and most critical task of adolescence.

A Way of Traveling versus a Place of Arrival

Sociologist Jeffrey Arnett claims that, in the early twenty-first century, young people in their late teens and early twenties view the "meaning and value of becoming an adult" as "a closing of doors—the end of independence, the end of spontaneity, the end of a sense of wide-open possibilities," and so, Arnett asserts, they are more reluctant to claim adult status than was true in the mid-twentieth century.[6] Perhaps such reluctance by adolescents is poorly grounded, for this perception of adult status as stasis and finality is not the lived reality of adults. Adulthood is not a place of arrival, achieved once and for all of life, or a line to be crossed by a specific age. Rather, as we age, the responsibilities of adulthood pile up unbidden. They do not wait until we feel ready. Regardless of our acquisition of fixed external markers (e.g., a license to drive, drink, or get married), adulthood is shaped by the *expectation* of our ability to be responsible in and to our relationships for ourselves and others—frequently without specific request or assent. These relationships may be with children in our care, but they may also be with employees, coworkers, family members, roommates, classmates, and even ourselves. Rather than something at which humans arrive, having accomplished given external criteria, adulthood is something into which we find ourselves moving, with steps advancing and retreating in turn. It is an incremental experience, even when circumstances plunge us into the unexpected; just because we have given birth to a child or had our parents pass away does not mean we quickly assume and master qualities of adult responsibility. Rather, once we begin to pick up the relational capacities of adulthood, they are things we both master and fail to master for the remainder of our lives. Furthermore, once someone has gained the relational capacities to function as an adult, that does not mean she will never again act in a way that is childish (e.g., self-focused or irresponsible) or childlike (e.g., eating ice cream out of the carton).[7] Likewise, even if someone wishes to forestall the obligations of adulthood by avoiding responsibility, her inaction may still have consequences for herself or others.

Reflecting the slow, back-and-forth nature of this shift, our language is fluid and changes incrementally in reference to individuals and context. At one instance in any given setting, we are calling an eighteen-year-old an adolescent and at another moment we are calling her a young adult. While more frequently seen at eighteen, that same shifting reference can also be used when the individual is sixteen or twenty-six; language usage depends on context and intention, not only on the age of the individual. This also demonstrates how language shapes what it names; our use of the terms in these diverse ways in different settings impacts what we recognize in the subject and how she sees herself.[8]

An Interpreted and Negotiated Status

Having argued that it is the *expectation of responsibility* that shapes much of adulthood, it remains to be determined *to whom* and *for what* must one be responsible to be considered adult. The answer to that question is not determined by the individual alone but is interpreted and negotiated between the individual and the multiple relationships within the context of the specific social surround. For example, someone may say, "I'm an adult because I pay my own bills." That is commendable and may seem a fair interpretation on her part. However, if it is expected that she is to pay for the expenses of her dependent children and she fails to meet that obligation, then she is failing in her interpretation of and her responsibility to her role as an adult.

For another example, it might be expected among European Americans that children must move out of their parents' home to be considered adult, but that same expectation is not a part of other cultural groupings, especially those of recent immigrants from Asia or Latin America.[9] The expectation of a young person as an adult might be that they remain in the family home while contributing to household obligations. Similarly, expectations of full-time employment or having completed one's education to be considered adult do not make sense when training for fields that require extended education but also tremendous responsibility (e.g., medicine). In each of these situations, responsibilities are interpreted and negotiated among those involved.

Another factor in the interpretation and negotiation is the *ability* of the individual to meet the surrounding expectations. There is no perfect human; we all have different abilities and disabilities, rendering us differently able to meet the challenges of living in the world.

One person, because of their significant ability, may come to be the "go to person" in a community, and asked to take on more of certain leadership responsibilities because of that ability. Likewise, someone with an acknowledged limitation may have to negotiate with others about how certain basic responsibilities relative to that limitation will be met.[10] In both cases, meeting the expectations of adulthood are not predetermined or automatically set, but interpreted and negotiated within a context. Because expectations are contextually determined, they are also changeable as circumstances necessitate. Such is the case when a person ages and loses physical or cognitive capacities, necessitating the shifting of obligations to others. They are still adults even if they need to renegotiate their responsibilities. The specific expectations of adulthood are determined contextually.

Taking a Turn at the Helm

Adults are expected to make decisions, to act, and to be held accountable for their acts, but it does not mean those decisions are made in isolation or without consultation with trusted others. Adulthood makes diverse demands, requiring the development of internal capacities (self-consciousness and self-awareness; awareness and management of time, past and future), along with interpersonal skills (consultation, communication, vulnerability, and trust), as well as reflective capacities wherein one can bring all these together and weigh options. All these begin to be developed in adolescence and take years to refine and master. In fact, we are never finished.

This image of adulthood—one responsible within the context of relationships—is like the crew member aware of her role on the sailboat. An able crewmate must learn her role, communicate with others, and act in a reliable manner for the good of all. To be an adult is to be like an able crew, taking on responsibility for a task and performing it to the best of her ability. Sometimes adulthood is like being at the helm, where she is responsible for directing the lives of others. Of all the positions on a sailboat, the helm, where the boat is steered, usually requires the most responsibility. At the helm, one directs and coordinates the actions of other members of the crew. So, while the helmsperson does not do all the tasks that are involved with sailing, she is usually the source of direction for all those tasks. Thus, each crew member is responsible for their particular task, but when important things go wrong, the helmsperson is usually the person held account-able overall. All this requires her to be aware of the factors outside the boat that will affect its progress (wind, current, and various obstacles), be familiar with the handling of the boat (steering and sail trim), and be able to direct herself and the crew to meet those factors appropriately. While a position of great responsibility, it is not a solo operation. On the best sailboats, the helmsperson depends on the skills, observations, insights, and wisdom of the entire crew to assist in the decision-making process. Therefore, all crew members must be engaged and respon-sible. Frequently, there are circumstances wherein decisions have to be made quickly, but even then, in a crew that communicates well and respects one another's role, decisions can be made and executed by the helmsperson that reflect communal consideration. Likewise, the crew, familiar with the expectations of their role, can respond appropriately to the movements on the boat even if the helmsperson is unable to communicate explicit instructions.

Similarly, adulthood, while a place of responsibility, is not a solo operation. Adults benefit best from growing and drawing on the rela-tionships within which they function. Sometimes an individual plays a supportive role in a larger project, working with diverse others (e.g., on a sports team, family, work project). Sometimes, they are in leadership roles, where they must oversee and coordinate the combined efforts of multiple others (e.g., captain or coach, older sibling or parent, man-ager or employer). In each, she is called on to be aware of and work with others, attentive to the expectations of the setting and endeavor.

Made for Relating-in-Love

Conceiving of adulthood as the ability to act responsibly within the context of relationships is not only developmentally appropriate, it has theological warrant. As claimed in the first chapter, the human person, made in the image of God, is made in and for relationships. To identify the kind of relationship among human persons, I look to the trinitarian theology of Catherine LaCugna. In *God for Us*, she writes of the persons of the Trinity as "persons in communion." LaCugna begins by acknowledging the value of Jesuit theologian Karl Rahner's conception of the inseparability of the *economic* and *immanent* Trinity—meaning, what we know of God's action in the world for our lives and salvation (*economic*) cannot be different from what God is in Godself (*immanent*). She writes,

> Rahner's principle on the identity between the economic and immanent Trinity is itself derived from the economy of salvation. The personhood of Jesus Christ ("hypostatic union") who is God-with-us, discloses also God-with-God. The Incarnation thus is proof of the strict identity between God in the economy and God as such.[11]

This claim is valuable for many reasons, but primarily because it means that what we believe about the Trinity must cohere with what we see in the work of Jesus and the Spirit in the world. LaCugna extends the characteristics of the personhood of the Trinity to human personhood. But here she finds Rahner's argument for the relationality among persons—in the Trinity and between God and human persons—inadequate because of what she calls Rahner's inability to put aside the modernist Cartesian "idea of person as discrete self-consciousness."[12] She claims that since Rahner, theological exploration has benefited from the postmodern discourse in other fields of study that has gone "beyond the dualism and individualism of the Cartesian tradition by giving priority to" the various social realities that shape the individual person.[13] Naming four threads in her trinitarian theology, LaCugna argues that human salvation is found in "living as persons in communion, in right relationship."[14]

Her first thread is drawn from the work of philosopher John Macmurray, who claimed René Descartes's "turn to the subject" was a retreat from the world. She claims that for Macmurray, "the Self withdrawn into itself, into self-reflection, is neither a true self nor a true person," but rather, "the Self is an agent: it is what it does." It is "a person directed toward other persons....The Self can be a Self only in relation to other selves."[15] Central to his argument is recognizing that other selves are not simply objects in the Self's world, but also agents and subjects in their own right. It is the interaction among them, in given circumstances and environments, which shapes who they are.

LaCugna writes that according to Macmurray, "'I' am constituted a person only in reference to 'You.'"[16]

The value of Macmurray's contribution for our discussion is that it affirms the potential emptiness of the self-constituted Self. That is not to suggest that reflection and contemplation are dead-end pursuits. Rather, the Self without reference to others has the potential, first, to deny that our lives are shaped by our social worlds prior to our determination and reflection; second, to deny the impact our agency has on the lives of others; third, to deny the validity and fullness of others beyond their reference to us; and fourth, to claim that we can validly interpret ourselves and our world in isolation. For our purposes, Macmurray's claim for the Self in light of its relation to others supports the call for developing a relational capacity.

LaCugna's second thread is drawn from Orthodox theologian John Zizioulas, who helps identify the nature of human personhood. Zizioulas looks to the self-gift and self-communication of God in the persons of the Trinity as indicative of the essential nature of personhood: *free* and *ecstatic*. What we know of God is that God is always freely moving ecstatically, within Godself, and with and toward God's creation. God is always in relationship—in communion—with God's creation; otherwise creation would not be. The fact of creation shows the essential nature of God. LaCugna summarizes, "Only *in communion* can God be what God is, and only *as communion* can God be at all."[17] She notes that Zizioulas is not bound by Western conceptions of freedom, which posit freedom as "perfect self-possession." Rather, "for Zizioulas, freedom belongs to the arena of ecstasis and self-transcendence. Ultimately freedom...means conformity to the image of God in us."[18] When we conform to the image of God, we go beyond the limiting and limited concerns for our biological self-preservation to give ourselves as gift. LaCugna explains that the human as "creature cannot escape being limited," but when he freely gives himself in love, it is the power of God working within and through him that moves beyond the boundaries of his limitations.[19] For Zizioulas, that freedom is found in baptism wherein through Christ and the Spirit we discover "a new being-in-relation, a new capacity for self-transcendence...a genuine instance of freedom."[20] Here, we see the Orthodox concept of *theósis* (divinization), whereby the person is transformed through the power of God working in and through the human person. "The deified person, conformed to the person of Christ, is an authentic expression of ecstasis toward communion, and thus an icon of God's own mystery of communion which originates with the Father and subsists in Christ and the Spirit."[21]

For our discussion, the value of Zizioulas's theology of the person *as going out* to the other, not over and against the other, but as free gift, conforms to what we experience in God through Jesus Christ. It also places our best and highest purpose in the move out to the other while acknowledging that effort is made possible through grace, that is, God's work in and through the uniquely created person. Furthermore, Zizioulas's framing of freedom as being oneself and giving oneself generously (rather than freedom from obligations to others), is particularly pertinent to adolescents who are just beginning to recognize themselves as unique persons whose lives have consequence. In fact, Zizioulas's image of enthusiastic and generous self-gift is reflective of an adolescent's response to the felt experience of being loved. In the experience of love, what the adolescent has found for himself, he wishes to share with the world. This image of personhood stands in contrast to a cultural narrative that communicates to the adolescent that he is insufficient and inconsequential.

While Macmurray and Zizioulas "clearly break away from the extreme individualism of the Cartesian framework," neither of them offers a critique of problematic relationships. LaCugna argues that not every "configuration of persons-in-relation images God"; rather some are "antithetical to divine life."[22] So, for her third thread she turns to feminist and Latin American liberation theologians. They critique historical patterns of social inequality—whether gender based or race based—that have been supported by theological claims that hierarchical human relationships reflect God's proper relationship within God-self and with the world, and so all human relationships must remain strictly hierarchical. LaCugna looks to feminist theologian Patricia Wilson-Kastner, who retrieves the ancient trinitarian image of *perichórésis*. As LaCugna explains,

> *Perichórésis* means being-in-one-another, permeation without confusion....to be a divine person is to be *by nature* in relation to other persons. Each divine person is irresistibly drawn to the other, taking his/her existence from the other, containing the other in him/herself, while at the same time pouring self out into the other.[23]

This dynamic image of the persons of the Trinity provides, according to LaCugna, "a dynamic model of persons in communion based on mutuality and interdependence."[24] It is a dynamic model that invites the possibility of flow but is "essentially communal and mutual. The image is of a divine dance;" the dance partners are essential to one another and to the dance.[25] Brazilian theologian Leonardo Boff, like Wilson-Kastner, turns to the image of *perichóresis*, but, according to LaCugna, uses it to critique "cultural notions of personhood, community, society, and the church. Trinitarian communion is opposed to individualism, isolationism, and asocial personhood. Trinitarian communion is opposed to both liberal capitalism and socialism. The first depersonalizes persons by reducing them to a means of production, the second annuls differences among persons."[26] The relation between persons is essential and primary but does not detract from the individual. Rather, right relationship grounds each and all with and to one another for their mutual benefit.

This liberation perspective is valuable as we consider how adolescents are just beginning to see and value the social. Relationships are newly recognized and newly important. Yet amid this new awareness, adolescents often infer the cultural call to be "independent" as a demand to stand on their own, separate from others, and potentially to use others for their personal advancement. The pervasive cultural narrative of rugged individualism, while counterintuitive to their deeper desires, can convince adolescents that there is something wrong with their desires for deep connection and relationship. It can also compel them to believe that they should try to make it in this life without the help or companionship of others, that they should be able to make sense of the world on their own. Such conflicting messages and feelings can frustrate and anger the adolescent, potentially leading to self-destructive behaviors (e.g., binge drinking, self-harm, sexual promiscuity) or to lash out at others (e.g., violence, bullying). In contrast, the theological perspective provided by LaCugna offers a corrective to the cultural narrative; the desire among adolescents for meaningful relationships is right and appropriate. Furthermore, *perichóresis* offers an image of relationships without the threat of being consumed and lost; rather relationships offer the promise of being found, even saved.

The final thread LaCugna draws is from Roman Catholic and Orthodox theological ethics to speak of the nature of relationships. From the Orthodox, LaCugna draws again from the concept of *theósis*:

> *Theósis* means being conformed in our personal existence
> to God's personal existence, achieving right relationship
> and genuine communion in every aspect, at every level. Sin
> is broken relationship, the distortion of the image of God in
> us. Sin, in other words, disorders and fractures our capacity
> for communion. Salvation reestablishes the image of God
> in us, and restores right relationship throughout creation.[27]

While she values this concept of relationality as foundational for salvation, LaCugna charges that Orthodox ethics remain uncritical of relationships of inequality. She looks to Catholic ethicist Margaret Farley, who reminds us that the offer of oneself to another should be a free offering, not something coerced or obliged. Farley challenges the narrow interpretation of *agape* as self-sacrifice that has been frequently used to support subservient relationships as a model of Christian life. Reflecting on self-gift in the Trinity, Farley argues for a wider interpretation that she calls "actively receptive." LaCugna writes, "God the Father's relationship to the Son comprises infinite self-giving but also infinite self-receiving. The Son literally receives Sonship from the Father, and in this reception, gives back to and constitutes the Father to be what the Father is: begetter of the Son."[28] Mutuality and reciprocity are at the heart of this intradivine relationship of self-gift. By framing right relationships as mutual and reciprocal, we have an alternative to the instrumental or transactional model of human interactions that are found in children, but also prevalent within the wider culture.

As adolescents recognize and contribute more consciously to the relationships in their lives, it is important they appreciate that relationships are not win-or-lose transactions. In fact, one receives in the act of giving, and one's gracious receptivity is a gift to another. Likewise, right relationship does not imply an absolute or predetermined obligation of one toward another, of always giving or being subservient. Rather there is shared care and respect, given and received. Relational mutuality and reciprocity reflect the *perichóresis* named earlier and modeled in the Trinity; it is a back-and-forth that is dynamic and ever evolving, shaping and critiquing the relationship along the way. To sin is to deny or stifle that movement toward right relationship. To deny it is to move contrary to the nature of God at work in the relationship.

Conclusion

Maturation through adolescence, to recognize and live responsibly into relationships, is the growth for which the human person is made. Our faith in the trinitarian God informs us of the kind of relationships we envision. They are relationships where we give ourselves freely and generously, where we come to know ourselves as we come to know the other, where we respect and enjoy mutuality and justice, where we are found and valued. Within such relationships, we experience the grace of God's love for us and contribute to that loving grace for another. However, as discussed in part 1, the number of connections we have, the demands accumulated among them, and the dispatch with which we attend to those demands all work to undermine the necessary investment needed for attending well to our relationships. As a result, the practices of relating well are not consistently being learned today, and the grace of love discovered within those relationships is missed.

I am frequently asked where I learned to sail. The question indicates that people presume sailing is a learned skill and explicit instruction would have been necessary. The easy answer is I took a course at a yacht club. The fuller answer is that starting with the formal lessons, I learned to sail and race through the invitation and direction of several seasoned skippers. Each generously took me on board and taught me something new in each experience. I have taken my turn at the tiller several times now, have made mistakes, and learned to make corrections. Now I own a sailboat, but am *still* learning and am thankful for many generous sailors who share their skills and invest in my learning. I now appreciate that sailing is something I will never fully perfect, in large part because the factors are constantly in flux—wind, current, crew, weather, equipment—and so each moment is new.

Living as an adult and living into relationships is at least as challenging as sailing, if for no other reason than the conditions—people and circumstances—are constantly in flux. However, we seldom recognize the need for teaching the complex practices of living responsibly into relationships. Relating well is a skilled activity that, like sailing, is best learned in the company and guidance of attentive and careful instructors "on the water," within the stream of life's activities. Relating well does not necessarily require formal programs or curriculum. Instead, it requires relationships that help a young person learn *that* they are *in relationships*, and what those relationships demand or expect of them.

5

Discovering a Horizon

One of the biggest challenges of learning to sail is making sense of the observable conditions and knowing how to respond to them. For example, the movement of trees, flags, and the water's surface each tell you something about how strongly the wind is blowing and from which direction. Yet, even knowing what to look for does not mean you know how to appropriately interpret and respond. It takes years of practice and reliable direction from someone more skilled to get it right. Yet the novice sailor tends to keep his eyes in the boat. He knows the wind is what makes the boat go, but he is preoccupied with how he has the boat trimmed and seldom looks outside the boat to watch for the changes in the wind. Thus he cannot anticipate those conditions or take advantage of them. To him, wind shifts are a nuisance or a threat. If prompted, he will train his body to feel the boat's movement, thus allowing him to keep his eyes outside the boat. In this way, with time and instruction, he learns to read wind shifts, and is able to maximize his progress by anticipating and taking advantage of those shifts. Because he is looking outside the boat, he is able to interpret, anticipate, and respond to what can contribute to his progress.

Just as the novice sailor needs to look beyond the boat, so too the adolescent has to learn to look beyond himself to recognize and interpret his relationships accurately and act effectively. If adulthood is the capacity to live responsibly within the context of relationships, the challenge of adolescence is *growing the capacity* to do so. It is the relationships themselves that serve as the curriculum, the classroom, and the motivation for learning about the relating. Relationships communicate values, identity, sense of purpose for life, and place.[1] Thus relationships are central—not ancillary—to adolescent maturation. In this chapter, we argue that the relationships and relational settings are the places wherein we make sense of who we are. Here, ministers and educators should be attentive to the quality and nature of those relational spaces.

Looking beyond the Boat

As relationships within an adolescent's social world become more apparent to the adolescent, they also become more important. Thus fitting in with the individuals and groups in her world takes on new urgency and provides the motivation to learn what is expected for her to do so. She learns that her actions—and even inaction—can please or displease others. As a result, she begins to understand a sense of consequence for her actions; that her behavior matters to those who matter. And "those who matter" are those who hold some value for her, for paralleling the adolescent's newfound social awareness is an awareness of social value. This starts with the awareness that something extrinsically valuable can be gained by connection to these people; and this is usually interpreted in broad strokes. For the young adolescent (this happens for girls before boys), it is the recognition that there is an "in" group and everyone else. She does not decide what makes the "in" group valuable; even those in the "in" group do not decide that. Their value is just a given, determined by some unseen authority of coolness, imposing strict codes for compliance.[2] Yet she does know that her social value is determined in relation to the group.

Along with the group's social value is communicated some framework of values. This is accomplished through the group's *narratives* (stories it tells about itself) and *practices* (patterns of behaviors within the relationships). Whereas the narratives and the practices may be detectable or observable and therefore obvious, the values they communicate are more invisible. They are inferred from the narratives and practices. Like the sailor learning to look for the impact of the wind on the surface of the water, a task of adolescence is learning to recognize and interpret the more invisible values and intentions embedded in a community's practices and narratives, and to know how to respond. Our young adolescent learns to read various signs to figure out what is intended, expected, and valued. Things that were previously invisible or innocuous become visible and important: emotions, gestures, body language, words spoken and written, and—increasingly—emojis, punctuation, and other tools of social media.[3] Likewise, more enduring things, like clothing and possessions, are now filled with meaning and value beyond their utility.[4] Our young adolescent discovers that what is *in* with one crowd is decidedly *out* with another, whether it is clothing, music, or interests. Through the group's communication of favor or disfavor toward her actions, she perceives her value in light of those relationships or communities.

While we often think of adolescent identity formation as a move of independent self-construction, in fact the adolescent's sense of self is drawn from the group's value, narratives, and practices. Philosopher Charles Taylor writes,

> I am only a self in relation to certain interlocutors: in one way in relation to those conversation partners who are essential to my achieving self-definition; in another way in relation to those who are now crucial to my continuing grasp of languages of self-understanding—and of course, these classes may overlap. A self exists only within what I call "web of interlocution."[5]

Taylor is arguing that a sense of value and identity is not constructed out of nothing, freely determined by the author without reference to others. Rather it is drawn from those elements that already have value in the given social world. For example, it means that what is cool in one middle school may be different from what passes as cool in another school, but in each, those young adolescents know what's what. Essential to the young person is that she recognizes and interprets the signs correctly; and correctly means in line with the power brokers in that setting.

Developmental theorist Erik Erikson, who first named identity formation as an essential task of adolescence, also points to the social nature of an individual's identity. Within the formation of identity, the adolescent recognizes and aligns with something greater than herself. She develops "fidelity," which Erikson considers the "vital strength" of this stage.[6] The adolescent begins to cast her lot with those with whom she aligns, which also means she takes on their values; she participates in the narrative and practices of the group; and she speaks out on behalf of the group's values. Thus she interprets and takes on the values implied within each relational setting. Her ability to live by those values within that group contributes to her social capital as others within the group perceive her as a member. Furthermore, the group's values have the potential to place her life in a wider framework of meaning; they can tell her that her life matters for something—immediately and eternally. She is about something because the group is about something. Thus her participation contributes to her sense of personal worth and consequence.[7]

What starts in broad brushstrokes in early adolescence becomes nuanced over the next several years. The growing adolescent may come to see that the "cool kids" are not so cool, or at least affiliating with them is not as valuable as she once thought. She now begins to recognize that those who share her interests or laugh at her jokes (and not at her) are the ones she values. By the end of high school, we usually see her displaying less effort to fit into groups that "everyone else" holds as valuable. By then, she has begun to recognize that she can choose to be part of groups and relationships that hold value for her. We can see it in her choice to be a "band nerd" or "youth group kid" or any subgroup. Note that this choice, while seeming to be a choice to stand apart on her own, is really a choice to stand with a group that is outside the mainstream, but still a group of some sort that helps her name her sense of self. Similarly, the choice of college functions the same way. If she could choose a school, she will look for one wherein she feels she will fit. On campus tours, she may look to the student guides to figure out what it means to be a student there and to imagine herself on that campus. Once she gets to that campus, the process of fitting in begins again, but now with greater nuance and selection than was possible earlier, as she looks for groups with which she might align. At this stage of adolescence, the rules of membership remain largely outside her control, like hooking up or binge drinking.[8] However, she can decide, better than in middle school, which community and rules are valuable to her.

A similar evaluative process happens with her preexisting relationships, like family, church, and childhood friends. While it may seem like she's leaving them behind, she is just putting them at arm's length, far enough away so she might see them anew and judge them. For example, as she comes to see her family as distinct from other families, she notices everything about the family anew and starts to judge. Suddenly, favorite family activities, inside jokes, and unquestioned influence start being questioned, but not necessarily rejected. From arm's length she can decide what to do with the relationships with parents, siblings, and family at large. At one moment she skulks on the sidelines of family gatherings and the next enthusiastically dives into the middle. She will do the same with longtime friends and associations; in the past, these were simply givens of her life, chosen for her by others or by circumstance. Now she is making more conscious choices.

In all this, the recognition of communities, relationships, their narratives and practices offer her a horizon on which to imagine herself. She can claim that she is about something because they are about something. Philosopher Alasdair MacIntyre argues that our personal narratives are always composed from within the narratives of our communities and relationships. He writes, "I am not only accountable, I am one who can always ask others for an account, who can put others to the question. I am part of their story, as they are part of mine."[9] As the adolescent begins to discover who she is and where she is, she is finding herself standing amid relationships and commitments, embedded in values of a social surround. Even if she wishes to stand apart from those relationships and commitments, her self-definition is composed in contradistinction from those others. What makes adolescence different from childhood is that she is more conscious of the choices she is making; it is that same consciousness that increases her agency. Now she knows what she is doing and with whom she is doing it.

An Obscured Horizon

If it is natural for adolescents to begin to look beyond themselves to know how they should act, commit, and think of themselves, why do we not see greater evidence of commitment to communities and moral integrity among adolescents and young adults?[10] Why, rather, do we see an increase in anxiety, depression, and even suicide among adolescents? As the adolescent grows, he is naturally inclined to recognize and interpret his social surround. However, it is not automatic that he will move from an instrumental to a relational perspective, whereby he is considerate of others and his obligations to them. Such a transformation depends on what that social surround is communicating and how he is interacting with it. Consequently, while it is natural that your average adolescent will be able to recognize the values embedded in the surrounding culture, it is not automatic that those values will be prosocial or relationally oriented.

As argued in chapter 2, the United States' cultural narrative focuses on and privileges the individual's rights and freedoms.[11] Overlaid onto that narrative is another, very strong economic narrative that privileges marketability, choice, and acquisition.[12] Those two narratives, unchallenged by anything to the contrary, do not support a shift away from an instrumental perspective; rather they encourage it by focusing on the individual in competition with others. This is especially true for the adolescent who has no trustworthy person close at hand to challenge those narratives. On the one hand, the adolescent who easily succeeds within the current cultural narrative—she has money, social influence, the attention of others—is encouraged to get better at what works for her. As a result, she ages into an increasingly savvy, instrumental person. On the other hand, the adolescent who struggles to keep up within such a system—needing to compete for every advantage—may live in a constant state of seeking approval. The result for him may be depression, anxiety, and an always provisional sense of security. If neither adolescent has any substantial voices to offer compelling alternatives, each will likely remain on the path offered, hoping to succeed in this high-stakes competition, and not make the shift to a relational perspective.

The individualistic and market-based narratives also impact the adolescent's values. Those narratives never encourage her to think beyond herself so as to understand and care for others, especially others who are not like her. The only reason to attend to another is to serve her self-interest in that moment—to get her ahead or to avoid difficulty. She is not encouraged to alter the moral compass that she had as a child, whereby "true north" remains her self-interest; such is the nature of an instrumental perspective.[13] She acts as needed in a situation, but with no sense of integrity across situations. She follows the rules as given unless she can get away with doing what she really wants. She functions on a zero-sum system; if I win, you lose and if you win, I lose. The world is necessarily made of winners and losers. Other people are either impediments to or avenues toward her goal. She is accustomed to using others and being used by others, like a commodity seeking to attain and hold value. It is how the game is played. Therefore, she may feel bad about using people, but she feels no sense of responsibility toward others; like her, they too should be looking for and working toward their own self-interest. An ironic example of a savvy instrumental actor is one who uses the language and practices of relationship and romance, but whose underlying behavior indicates she really has no sense of concern for the other but for her own advancement; she pursues community service to build her resume, not to serve those in need.

The individualistic and economic narrative also suggests a short-sighted sense of purpose. Educational psychologist William Damon argues that "the single greatest barrier to youngsters finding their paths to purpose is the fixation on short horizons that infuses cultural messages sent to young people today."[14] Damon describes purpose as "a stable and generalized intention to accomplish something that is at the same time meaningful to the self and consequential for the world beyond the self."[15] By fixating on the "short horizons" offered within the cultural narratives, the adolescent is not compelled to imagine her life within a wider framework of meaning. Rather, the messages are "convincing many young people to exert energetic (sometimes frantic) efforts in pursuit of achievement…unconnected to ultimate concerns."[16] All of which, Damon argues, leaves the young person anxious, exhausted, and hopeless.

Functioning with short horizons is akin to sailing in fog, wherein you can only see a short distance in any direction. If you are blithely unaware of anything beyond what is seen, you may sail along attending only to your own progress without any sense of direction or potential collision. If you suspect that there is something beyond the fog, but become anxiously inattentive, you may lose your course or suddenly collide with hidden obstacles. When sailing in fog, it is important to remain quietly vigilant, listening for what is unseen and attentive to any signs that help you find your bearings.

Apprenticing to an Able Skipper

We have argued that the social world surrounding the adolescent is the stuff from which he draws his values and makes sense of his life. We have also seen that without compelling reason to do otherwise, the contemporary narrative encourages him to continue viewing the world instrumentally. For the adolescent to move from the self-interested stance of the child, something must draw him to do so; it is not something to which he is likely to come to on his own. Therefore, the social surround and the quality of his relationships matter. If the adolescent is to recognize and engage in the world relationally, he needs to be surrounded by relationships that call him to notice and pay attention to the world outside himself. Sufficiently compelling relationships will draw him to recognize the existence of his relationships and their importance to him. Furthermore, if we are to help him grow the capacity for relationality as described in chapter 4—responsible, freely giving, nonhierarchical, and mutual—those relationships need to embody such relationality.

According to researchers in adolescent development, the single most consistent factor among adolescents who display a prosocial sense of purpose is relationships with nonfamily adults who believe in them, suggest direction, and support them in achieving their goals.[17] Evidence indicates that the centrality of such relationships cuts across economic, racial, and ethnic lines.[18] In other words, some relationships are able to draw adolescents to look up from themselves and out to the world. These may be referred to as mentoring relationships or what I refer to as robust relationships.[19] By *robust* I mean relationships wherein you are known well and loved fully. It is a relationship that the adolescent cannot easily ignore, but that over time develops an intrinsic value. A robust relationship invites the adolescent to discover himself as a person, unique and valuable, by drawing him into attentive relationships with another. It allows him to take chances and be vulnerable for the sake of new discoveries both in himself and in the world.

Robust relationships with adults who are not the adolescent's parents are important to the adolescent's growth because the job of raising adolescents is bigger than can be expected of parents alone. In fact, the parent-child relationship, while terribly important, is already emotionally weighted, making it difficult for sons and daughters to hear their parent's voice without judgment attached. Frequently, adolescents assume that parents are "supposed to" love and encourage them, so their parents' words are frequently dismissed as unreliable.[20] Likewise, it is difficult for parents to reflect on their children's lives with disinterest. While parents may play many roles in their children's lives, one role they cannot play is not-the-parent. They know that, as do their children. Rather, it takes the efforts of a few other important adults who know the adolescent well and can offer credible perspective.[21] Therefore, it is important for parents to recognize the value of other adults in their children's lives and invite or allow those adults to engage with their children in ongoing and meaningful ways.

For a robust relationship to develop, there needs to be opportunity, but there must also be interest from the adolescent. The relationship must be with someone he cannot ignore or dismiss. As suggested earlier, the adolescent needs to perceive some sense of value in staying connected to that adult, to pay attention to the adult despite critique. At first the motivation for paying attention will probably be extrinsic, like a relative famous for generous birthday gifts, or like the coach of the soccer team on which the adolescent wishes to get playing time. In either case, it is someone not easily ignored or dismissed; someone who will be around and has a right to be heard.

For him to move from the instrumental engagement of childhood toward the relational capacity of adulthood, it is important that the adolescent recognize his impact on others. A robust relationship with an adult can assist the adolescent to look beyond himself in meaningful ways. It can draw the youth to pay attention to others, to recognize his agency and consequence in the world. In multiple, diverse ways, this adult communicates to the adolescent, "If you want to hang with me, you have got to stop being so self-involved." The learning is gradual, with adults building on what educator Lev Vygotsky calls the "zone of proximal development";[22] recognizing what the adolescent can do and see, the adult helps them to see and do whatever is next. It is the aunt who points out that his rudeness to his younger brother is what caused his mother to be upset with him and suggests that he reconcile with his brother. Or it is the coach explaining that he is not getting more playing time because his focus on his own play means he is not passing to his teammates. But the messages should not be all negative. It is also important to point to the positive consequences, to which the adolescent may be equally blind. It is the aunt noticing his patience with his younger brother or the coach noticing that teammates look to him for leadership. Either way, the adult's critique and praise must be grounded in reality, not fake or pro forma. In this way, the adult's perspective assists the adolescent to recognize his agency in the relationships and his interpretation of his world.

Part of the growing challenge for the adolescent is to begin to appreciate others as *other*, with interests, concerns, and hopes of their own. It is more likely the adolescent will assume that others share his perspective, and so he must learn to recognize and interpret what others intend. To align with what another intends requires conversational engagement between the adolescent and the other person. As described by philosopher Hans-Georg Gadamer, appropriate interpretation requires him to test his presumptions against what he encounters in the conversation with the other.[23] For example, he may assume that his soccer coach wants to win at all costs. It would take the coach explaining that while winning is a goal, the coach's greater concern is to create a cohesive and enjoyable team on which all get to grow and contribute. In fact, the coach may argue that for the team to succeed, all of its members need to work together. Successful understanding of the other and of the relationship is not something the adolescent can guess at alone. Rather, proper understanding is accomplished in the back-and-forth process of inquiring, misunderstanding, and building a new understanding. This is not a one-way instruction but a mutual give-and-take whereby both come to a more expansive insight together—what Gadamer refers to as a "fusion of horizons."[24] Creating the relational space for this back-and-forth conversation reflects the *perichórésis* of relationality, the back-and-forth of the dance among those in relationship.

Yet the learning process is slow, filled with missteps along the way. Correct interpretation is learned slowly over time with practice and redirection.[25] Therefore, room must be allowed for the growing adolescent to learn and recover from the mistakes he will make. For the adolescent to grow, there needs to be both consequence and forgiveness. This is what Erikson meant by "moratorium," that the responsibility carried by the adolescent should not be so great as to be devastating should he fail to meet it.[26] However, failure should not be consequence-free, otherwise he will neither recognize his agency in relationship with others, nor how to endure and survive in the face of mistakes. Thus forgiveness and reconciliation need to be exhibited in the relationship; as such, it reflects ongoing giving and receiving that is central to relationality. Again, the necessity of trusted and trustworthy others who communicate with him truthfully cannot be overemphasized. If others dismiss him when he is wrong, or turn away, afraid to get involved, he will likely misattribute or fail to notice his impact.

Learning to Read the Wind

In time, the adolescent's awareness of value will shift. First, as noted earlier, she begins by recognizing an extrinsic value in the person whose critique and instruction she is willing to endure. But in time, she may find intrinsic value in the relationship itself. It will take time for her to recognize that maintaining and growing a relationship requires something different from the simple reciprocity she understood as a child ("Sometimes I get my way; other times you get yours."). She will need someone to show her that the relationship itself requires a deeper reciprocity for the good of the relationship itself ("Sometimes I don't get my way and you don't get yours, but we get what we need for us."). Her ability to recognize the relationship as such and attend to its health and vitality demonstrates a significant growth over her capacity as a child. It is a major step toward taking responsibility, not just for herself, but also for her role in the relationship. This is how she comes to recognize and contribute to the common good, that which is neither you nor I, but us and we.[27] But she is unlikely to make that imaginative leap if not called and directed to do so by someone else who already recognizes it. If she values the other person—and the other asks—the adolescent will come to see that relationship between them for the sake of staying in relationship with the other. The robust relationship becomes what developmental theorist Robert Kegan calls a "holding environment," a space that promotes growth by balancing support and challenge.[28]

Value can also be understood in yet another way. As the adolescent finds intrinsic value in the relationship, she begins to recognize and take on the values embodied in the relationship, like truthfulness, commitment, and consideration. But such values tend to be more invisible until the adolescent learns to look. When sailing, to advance the boat, we must pay attention to the invisible force of the wind—its direction and velocity. Yet direction and velocity are constantly variable, from day to day, but also even from moment to moment. Our ability to be aware of and interpret those factors and to work amid their shifts is essential for moving the boat effectively. We need to learn to read the invisible wind by looking to its observable impact—the feeling on the skin, the influence on the sails, and the changes on the surface of the water. Interpreting the wind's movement and knowing

70

what to do in response takes time and attention to learn and master. So, it is through learning to recognize and act on the values in any given setting. They are embedded in the narratives and practices of a setting but remain invisible until we learn to read them.

Over time, the narratives and relational practices embodied within the robust relationship provide a meaningful and credible horizon upon which the adolescent might imagine her life. Through the modeling, direct instruction, and example of a trustworthy adult, the adolescent can come to imagine how her life might contribute to a greater sense of purpose. Sharon Daloz Parks notes that mentoring relationships recognize, support, challenge, and inspire young people into a broader sense of purpose. She argues that these relationships create an imaginative space whereby the young person can come to see her life in more expansive and purposeful ways.[29] A robust relationship, by offering both praise and critique, hopes and limitations, helps the adolescent gain a greater sense of her place in the world. Through the relationship, she discovers her value and purpose as a unique person.

Finally, it is only when the adolescent begins to recognize the intrinsic value of relationships that she will come to understand sin as doing damage to persons and relationships. Theologian Catherine LaCugna ties sin to the discussion of *theósis*:

> *Theósis* means conforming our personal existence to God's personal existence, achieving right relationship in every respect, at every level. Sin is broken relationship, the distortion of the image of God in us. Sin, in other words, disorders and fractures our capacity for communion. Salvation reestablishes the image of God in us, and restores right relationship throughout creation.[30]

If the adolescent, on the one hand, does not recognize relationships, and the personhood generated therein, she will be limited to seeing sins as an arbitrary list of behaviors to avoid. On the other hand, when she comes to recognize the intrinsic value of relationships, she can more intentionally and creatively contribute to their flourishing and recognize when she is undermining them.

The Communion of Saints

As children, we can get away with being thoughtless and short-sighted because it is within the limits of children to respond to the world as it suits their immediate needs. As we age into adolescence toward mature adulthood, we are expected to be considerate of others—even those people we do not like, to anticipate behaviors and responses from others, and act in a way that reflects mutual consideration. We are expected to take on greater responsibilities for the relationships of which we are a part, both by those older and by age peers. It is through the growth of adolescence that we gain the capacities to recognize ourselves, our relationships, and consciously give ourselves and receive others in relationship. This is not something learned in isolation, but among trusted and trustworthy companions. It is not learned once and for all time, but is grown into and practiced for the remainder of life.

It may seem like a double bind. We need good relationships to learn to relate well; we need to relate well to form good relationships. Which comes first? Throughout this period of maturation, the onus—particularly that of teaching how to be in relationships, interpret contexts, and be responsible—rests on the more mature adults within the adolescent's world. To do that job well, those adults need to have sufficient rapport with the young person to be a credible voice for such lessons. However, the young person may be under the impression that they should be able to attain the skills of adulthood on their own and should not reach out to mature adults for help. So let us finish the line of thought. On the individual level, it rests on the shoulders of adults to develop credible and robust relationships with younger people to share with them the skills of relating well. On the structural level, it takes community leaders—educators and ministers—to create environments whereby robust relationships are likely to be initiated and grown among the individuals therein.

The discussion has focused on individual relationships, and they are at the heart of the matter for the individual adolescent. But let us finish by turning to the community. The role for the church is to create the spaces wherein robust relationships are promoted, for such is the work of the Holy Spirit. LaCugna writes,

The goal of Christian community, constituted by the Spirit in union with Jesus Christ, is to provide a place in which everyone is accepted as an ineffable, unique, and unrepeatable image of God, irrespective of how the dignity of a person might otherwise be determined: level of intelligence, political correctness, physical beauty, monetary value. The communion of persons, however, remains the context of personhood. The community of Jesus Christ is the one gathering place in which persons are to be accepted and valued unconditionally, as equal partners in the divine dance.[31]

The Christian community, in its narratives, practices, and ancient wisdom, offers a meaningful horizon upon which the adolescent can learn about love. Giving access to that collective wisdom may be the primary gift we can offer adolescents. Yet more importantly, the Christian community also offers itself, the communion of saints, both living and historic. As a communion of saints, we serve as companions in relating and offer ourselves in relationship, living lives of love and meaning as we invite them to do the same. By opening ourselves up to adolescents in loving, robust relationships, we help them discover the gift of their own lives that God has offered to and through them, and we help them find ways to give that gift to the world. Our response as ecclesial communities is the focus of part 4.

Part Three

JOINING OTHERS ON BOARD

We might presume that the junior sailor graduates from the little *Optimist* to sail alone on a larger boat. That presumption would be in line with the dominant cultural narrative of independence named in chapter 2. However, that narrative ignores the fact that the young sailor was never sailing alone, even if no one was in the boat with her. Like a child ignorant of the efforts of those around her to keep her safe, the young sailor was unaware of what mature supervisors were doing on her behalf. Now that she has gained some basic skills, our young sailor graduates to sailing on larger, more complicated boats, with other sailors.

The growth through adolescence is something like joining on board a larger boat. To be a crew member is to contribute responsibly with others to the advancement of the larger project. It is to recognize what is expected in the role; it is to respond as needed, to take initiative, with concern for the safety and endeavor of the boat; it is to read the changing variables of the setting, anticipate expectations, and understand what all that means for one's own action. Thus, to become crew is to think and act increasingly interdependently, reliably, with consideration for how that thinking and acting impacts the whole crew. In time, a good crew member can be relied upon to fulfill obligations, anticipate needs, and plan for action without constant express instruction. It takes years to learn how to be a proficient crew, mastering multiple tasks on board. Such a crew member is then able to move from boat to boat, skipper to skipper, yet know how and when to act effectively and responsibly.

Similarly, the maturing adolescent needs to recognize that she is part of larger communities and relationships to which she needs to become a reliable contributor. No longer blindly assuming that someone else will take care of everything, the adolescent needs to become aware of others, contribute as expected and needed, take responsibility, and think and act reliably. Like a crew member joining a larger boat, the adolescent is learning to be a reliable and interdependent actor on behalf of a community in a larger, more complicated setting.

The capacities of recognizing, reflecting, and acting are first possible in the early teenage years and are developed throughout the long years of adolescence, if properly prompted. They are never outgrown but are refined with time, opportunity, and practice through adulthood. In chapter 6, we describe the cognitive development that is possible over the adolescent trajectory to give a dynamic sense of what is possible for the adolescent. In chapter 7, we describe how relationships are themselves what trigger the relational capacities. We close this part with a theological discussion of how God prompts the adolescent to be open to the presence and the movement of God within herself and in others.

6

Rigging a Larger Boat

Today, the most common sailboat is the sloop, with a mainsail and jib. The two sails of the sloop design allow for more sail surface than a single-sail boat without the need for a taller mast. Because the wind interacts with two sails differently than with one, it allows the boat to sail faster than single-sail boats and closer to the wind.[1] However, the added sail creates a more complex sailing experience in which the sailors need to pay attention to the interaction of the wind between the two sails. Sailing a sloop is a jump in complexity, not just capacity, requiring new skills that were not needed on the little *Opti*. Similarly, the growth that is possible through adolescence is not just a growth in capacity but also in complexity. Adolescents are not just expected to understand more of what they understood as children; the world expects them to understand what they know differently. Like the sailor who must learn that if you adjust one sail you have to adjust the other, the adolescent must begin to recognize the relationship and impact between things, whether those things are ideas, people, or values. In this chapter, we name the neurobiological changes during a person's teens and twenties that make it possible to see the world with greater complexity, thus to relate to the world differently than is possible in childhood. We then present a cognitive developmental framework by which we can better recognize the maturation process. This discussion is continued in chapter 7, wherein we argue that robust relationships assist adolescents in making this developmental shift.

Standing Rigging²

Recent neurobiological studies of children and adolescents have found that the human brain undergoes a second major period of growth and organization that lasts through the second decade of life and into the third.³ These changes provide the young person with new cognitive tools that enable a qualitatively different engagement with the world than is possible in childhood.⁴ The most dramatic changes happen during the teenage years and then gain refinement through the twenties. Understanding what these changes are and how they impact the life of the growing adolescent can give us a greater appreciation of the dynamic possibilities of this time and why maturing to adulthood is so complex. In this section, we briefly examine that growth process, highlight some of the changes happening within regions of the brain (the *frontal cortex*, the *amygdala*, the *corpus callosum*, and the *cerebellum*) during this period, and identify the impact this development has on how the adolescent can see and engage in the world.

From its earliest stages in life, the human brain matures from its base (the brain stem), which controls basic bodily functions (e.g., heartbeat, breathing), to its top front (the cortex), which is responsible for complex reasoning (e.g., problem solving, executive functioning, and long-term planning). Research reveals that the brain does not come to full maturity until the early to mid-twenties, at which time it resembles the adult brain. The last steps of the brain's maturation happen through the course of adolescence, during which time the brain gains plasticity, increasing the potential for learning and working in new ways. Plasticity, regarding the adolescent brain, refers to its ability to be molded and reshaped before setting into a "more fixed form" of the adult brain.⁵ It begins just prior to puberty, when there is a burst of new growth in the brain's grey matter, which is made up of brain cells (neurons) and the connections among those cells (synapses). This addition is particularly dramatic in the prefrontal cortex. The new growth anticipates changes in how the brain will function overall; previously underused regions of the brain will mature and processing centers will shift. Over the course of the next ten or more years, the initial growth spurt is followed by an organization of that grey matter. All these changes enable the growing person to function anew in the world; it allows for more complex ideation, better problem solving, better recognition and processing of stimuli, and greater fluidity in thought. These changes contribute to one's greater ability to function independently in the world, less reliant on parents or others for direction, and more able to determine an appropriate course of action for oneself.

However, there is nothing inevitable about the organization of these new cells and their connections; besides genetic factors, organization is determined in large part by use and environment. Therefore, stressors, challenges, nutrition, alcohol and drugs, sleep, cognitive and emotional supports, as well as trauma each have an impact on how the brain is used and develops.[6] Following the years of increase and organization, there is an eventual decrease in grey matter. Neurons and neural pathways that get used, especially repeatedly, get strengthened and protected, while those that do not are eventually pruned away.[7] Neuroscientist Jay Giedd speaks of the "use it or lose it" principle.[8] The pruning process makes for a more efficient brain in that it does not maintain unused resources, while those paths that are used become quicker and more reliable. Like the rest of the body's need for practice to master and refine movement, new brain patterns require repeated usage to become fluid. By the mid to late twenties, the window of opportunity for dramatic learning and change is closing; the brain is losing its adolescent plasticity as it becomes more committed to the shape it has now taken. This means that those in their teen years and even twenties are in a time of tremendous possibility in terms of growth and refinement of cognitive skills, or a time of missed opportunity.

Let us consider this growth with some specificity. Perhaps the most dramatic change in the adolescent brain is that the *frontal cortex* matures and is increasingly called into use. The cortex is the region of the brain that allows for ideation and abstraction. It is often referred to as "the CEO" of the brain because of its role in executive functioning: generating ideas, problem-solving, decision-making, and long-range planning. With the newly developing and organizing frontal cortex, the adolescent becomes more reliant on it for perception and cognition than was possible in childhood. The adolescent becomes less dependent on the concrete and is newly able to recognize and think in terms of themes and values—connections shared between concrete elements. With the development of the frontal cortex, he becomes newly able to recognize time past and time future, which enables the development of long-term cause and effect, as well as a sense of history, imagination, and long-range planning. The development of the frontal cortex allows for self-consciousness; the adolescent begins to see himself as thinking and feeling.

As the teenage brain becomes more dependent on the frontal cortex for making decisions, it becomes less dependent on the *amygdala*, the region in the center of the brain that processes emotion. The amygdala is the primary location for decision-making for the growing child. It allows the child to make quick responses to environmental cues, which is essential for keeping safe in the face of perceived threats. The early adolescent's continued dependence on the amygdala, coupled with a nascent capacity for self-consciousness made possible by the frontal cortex, contributes to making early adolescence seem very emotion laden. They are experiencing new emotions, especially as related to their social engagements, while increasingly self-conscious about experiencing emotions.

Since emotional expressions are widely varied among humans, it takes time for the adolescent to appropriately interpret and respond to them.[9] Research shows that young adolescents, who are still processing emotion-laden information primarily through the amygdala, are poor interpreters of their world. They tend to read emotional cues and quickly respond to situations before they have noticed more subtle details. As a result, they frequently misinterpret and react inappropriately to adult intentions and expectations.[10] On their side, adults — particularly parents — are often mystified and frustrated when the adolescent in their life accuses them of being angry when the adults were in fact feeling concern or distress or puzzlement. Unfortunately, adults often respond poorly to the teen's misdiagnosis and the situation escalates. Recognizing the growth processes the adolescent is undergoing may give the adult some appreciation for what is happening at moments like this. The adult then may create a nonanxious space to suggest an alternate interpretation to the adolescent. By doing so, not only does the situation not escalate, but the adolescent is assisted in imagining the adult's perspective.

With the development and use of the frontal cortex, adolescents become more capable of greater reflection on what they experience. And with some coaching, they can learn to take the time to see more and make better sense of what they see. Eventually, the decision-making process becomes more considered and less tied to emotional or gut responses. This shift takes time and is uneven over the years, resulting in thoughtful responses at one moment and incongruent outbursts at the next. Moving reactions away from the amygdala and to the cortex does not mean that emotions eventually become unimportant in decision-making. Rather, it becomes more possible for emotions to inform the decision-making process instead of drive it. Emotions become something the growing adolescent can think about and consider, rather than something to which they simply react. But we can all appreciate that when we are tired or frustrated, it is easier and quicker to react emotionally rather than thoughtfully. Thoughtful responses almost always take extra effort, so patience with oneself and others becomes an important virtue in the maturation process.

Concurrently, the linkage across the brain hemispheres—the *corpus callosum*—develops, making communication across spheres of the brain more sophisticated and supple.[11] The well-connected brain is better able to access information across regions of the brain and make new sense of that information. The development of the *corpus callosum* better enables the adolescent to make connections across intelligences as never before and contributes to a sense of systemic or thematic thinking. Finally, the *cerebellum*, long associated with physical coordination, has been found to assist the brain in "higher cognitive functions" such as complex math.[12] Its growth relates to physical activity, indicating that physical movement and stimulation contribute to the brain's functioning overall. In a tangible way, we can appreciate how coordinated, supple thinking mirrors how the adolescent body takes time to develop physical coordination and refined movement.

This neurobiological research should not be assumed to answer all our questions about the growing adolescent, nor do I use it to argue for some neurobiological determinism.[13] However, it does help us recognize the lively changes, previously unseen, happening within the brain at this stage of life. It helps us appreciate what is going on inside the adolescent that makes the challenge of growing to maturity possible and real. In other words, the adolescent brain is a growing tool by which adolescents are newly able to see more and make sense of what they see than was previously possible. Furthermore, this development does not happen like an on-off switch. Rather, these capacities, once initiated, take several years to refine, enhance, and reliably use, which means increased capacity in cognition can be first observed in the early teen years but continue well into one's twenties, just as the world's expectations of them become greater and more complex.

The Gift of Self-Consciousness

Perhaps one of the first obvious and dramatic changes initiated with the development of the frontal cortex is the development of self-consciousness; the ability to see oneself as *seeing* and *being seen*. While a child may behave as if she is the center of the universe, she is not self-conscious about doing so. With adolescence comes the ability to *see herself as* acting, seeing, and thinking. The shift takes time; in her early teen years, she still behaves as if she is the center of the universe, but she now believes everyone is watching and judging her just as she is watching and judging herself. This usually causes her to appear particularly awkward and self-centered. Psychologist David Elkind describes the phenomenon as the teen's "imaginary audience:" "[Early teens] assume that everyone around them is preoccupied with the same subject that engrosses them: namely, themselves."[14] This obvious self-consciousness is more visible in some adolescents than others, and tends to happen earlier for girls than for boys.

We may recall this early self-consciousness in our lives as a pain-ful and perhaps pointless moment. While we may wish it away as too dreadful to endure, we might look at it as a valuable sign of growth. The assumption that others are watching becomes an important con-tributor to how the growing adolescent begins to perceive that she is a person in relationship with people as complex as she is discovering herself to be—with emotions, opinions, and ideas. Self-consciousness is a sign that the adolescent is beginning to disembed from her childish frame of reference (I am at the center of a universe of fixed objects) toward a more complex frame of reference (I am amid others who are looking back at me). With self-consciousness, she begins to recognize that her feeling, thinking, and acting can be seen by others just as she begins to see them. In time, she also begins to grant to others what she recognizes for herself: that others are not fixed entities or extensions of her, but they possess feelings, thoughts, and acts that are independent of but impact her. Eventually, she can recognize that distinct from herself and from the other is the *relationship* that exists between them. Thus, in adolescence, she *can begin* to recognize that she has rela-tionships with herself and with others.[15] Once such recognition has begun, it can take years to fully appreciate and act upon the various relationships in her life with real sensibility. She is at the beginning of

82

an essential growth process, moving from seeing the world *instrumentally* to the beginning of *relational* awareness, all made possible by the development of her frontal cortex. The growth of relational awareness means she can recognize that there *are others* outside herself; they are not just instrumental actors, but full human persons. Furthermore, she may recognize she is *in relationship* with these others, with God, and even with herself. She can begin to recognize mutuality—that what she does or fails to do impacts what others see and think about her; that her actions have consequences beyond the immediate.

Self-consciousness—seeing that she is seen by others—is the growth that makes it possible for her to begin to develop her relational capacity. However, if not supported and challenged to think beyond her self-concern, this self-consciousness remains self-centeredness and she will continue to engage in the world instrumentally. More is said about how to support and challenge this growth in the next chapter. For the moment, we suggest only that the young person's ability to recognize the relationships in her life *as* relationships shapes her understanding of and her engagement in those relational contexts. With the neurological developments of adolescence comes a new capacity for her to see relationships, recognize their contextual expectations, respond, and recognize the longer-term consequences of her responses. Each of these tasks—self-seeing, seeing the other, seeing the relationship between, seeing her agency—are overlapping and interrelated yet distinct tasks potentially accomplished in adolescence. Such tasks were not possible for her during childhood. If she can take advantage of the potential for relational awareness throughout adolescence, she will see and make sense of so much more, she will gain greater freedom and independence in her ability to respond appropriately. She will gain a sense of where and how she fits into her world.

Running Rigging[16]

A sailing sloop can range in size from twelve feet to over forty feet, but the basic design remains the same: single mast, mainsail, and jib. The running rigging for each remains basically the same: jib sheet, main sheet, and jib and main halyards. However, the larger the sails become, the longer and heavier the lines that hold and control those sails (halyard and sheets) become. For a sailor to handle those longer, heavier lines, the lines are run back and forth through a series of pulleys, called blocks, each of which reduces the strain on the lines and so makes them easier for the sailor to handle. The visual effect, though, is significant. On a small boat, it is easy to see the four lines and determine what they do. However, on a larger sloop, those same lines are traversing back and forth between multiple blocks, so it may be difficult to identify the four. The complexity can be confusing; it takes time to recognize what is there.

Similarly, in early adolescence the young person can come to appreciate the connection among distinct others (like parents and friends) such that she changes from seeing them instrumentally and begins recognizing the relationship that connects her to them. She can come to recognize and appropriately manipulate the reciprocal dynamics of the relationship to accomplish mutually beneficial ends. However, it can take years to learn to recognize the complexity of relational connections as they pass through increasingly complex interchanges (like families and organizations). Thus the recognition and capacity to respond that begins in the early teens may not come to refinement and complexity until well into one's twenties and beyond. Through those years, it takes effort for the relationship complexity to shift from obscure to obvious. Developmental theorist Robert Kegan describes this cognitive shift that is first possible in adolescence as the move from knowing "durable categories" (also *second-order* knowing) to "cross-categorical" (or *third-order*) knowing. It is not simply a shift in capacity but in complexity, like moving from one sail to two; it is not simply what one knows, but the connections among what one knows that comes into play.

According to Kegan, an older child is capable of recognizing and learning that the world is composed of knowable, concrete categories that have "durable, ongoing rules." "What is being demonstrated [in the older child] is the ability to construct a mental set, class, or category to order the things of one's experience (physical objects, other people, oneself, desires) as property-containing phenomena."[17] For example, when it comes to people, the child sees himself and other people as entities with their own intentions, feelings, and points of view. To navigate among others and their interests, the older child's focus is on meeting his self-interest, just as he presumes those others are functioning out of their self-interest. Thus the goal of the older child is to meet his self-serving objectives while working in concert with others, or at least not getting caught by others when his self-interest conflicts with theirs.[18] This ability of the older child to see things, others, and himself as stable and learnable (and not a product of his perception of or wishes for them) is a significant leap beyond the ability of small children. It allows the older child to be planful—if only on a limited basis—and relatively independent. It also allows him to master the likes and dislikes of those important to him, and it gives him the capacity to use that information constructively. In fact, the young person working out of "durable categories" can be savvy in playing to the self-interests of others to meet his own needs, for he assumes their highest goal is their own self-interest as it is his. So, he presumes the connections in his life should serve for their instrumental or transactional value. While I refer throughout this paragraph to the older child, this second-order capacity of limiting the world to the instrumental can still be the frame out of which many older adolescents and even adults continue to function; in fact, individuals can age and become quite savvy in their instrumental skills and never take on a relational capacity.[19]

According to Kegan, the growth out of second order toward third-order thinking is not automatic with age but brought about through a combination of internal capacities and external prompts and supports. Though naturally directed toward the self-interest of the young person, second-order knowing becomes a limitation as the young person grows into adolescence. For those around him, particularly adults, expect him to move from self-interest as a motivator to consideration and concern for others. They will *expect* him to subordinate his immediate self-interest for the interests of his relationships and be disappointed when he does not. For him to subordinate his self-interest requires him to recognize the relationships, identify the interests of the relationships, recognize that his actions have impact on them, subsume his immediate interests for the good of the relationship, and act accordingly. Each of these tasks is distinct, but interrelated and learnable tasks that contribute to his ability to act with consideration for others. Regarding this shift, Kegan's colleague, Eleanor Drago-Severson, notes,

> Other people are experienced not merely as resources to be
> used by the self but as sources of internal validation, orienta-
> tion, or authority. The self is identified with, or made up by,
> its relationship to other people (family, important friends,

supervisors, or colleagues) or ideas (religious, political, or philosophical ideologies).[20]

According to Kegan, all of this indicates a development beyond second order toward third-order, cross-categorical knowing.[21] Essentially, it is moving from an instrumental to a relational engagement with the world.

Self-consciousness can precipitate the recognition of relationships and their contexts. I see others seeing me. I begin to recognize that what I say, do, and think has an impact on how others see and respond to me. I begin to recognize reciprocity between myself and those around me. But for this to move beyond the capacity of second order, I need to learn not only that other people have their perspectives, but I need to be open to them and learn what they are. I need to see and take account of perspectives beyond my own, and factor for those perspectives when making decisions that affect them. In doing so, I begin to recognize how my thoughts and actions have an impact on others whether I intend them to or not. In other words, I must sufficiently remove myself from my interests and point of view to see those of another. In doing so, I recognize that there is something between us—a relationship—that is impacted by what each person holds or does independently. So my guiding questions become less inspired by immediate self-interest (Will I get caught?) and more by concern for what lies between us (Will this undermine the trust between us? Even if they never find out, is this who I want to be for them?). Kegan writes,

> These questions betoken the existence of a different way of being *in* one's involvements with others, that of orienting not just to what will happen to me or to my wants but what will happen to my bond or connection or relationship. Relationships thus move from being extrinsically valuable to being intrinsically valuable.[22]

Thus, Kegan describes the capacity to remove myself from my perspective and the presumption that everyone shares my perspective toward a capacity to see and make sense of others' perspectives alongside which mine is held. As such, my new perspective widens to include what was seen before (self-interest) but is now subsumed within a new framework (relational interests).

For example, Michelle is in tenth grade. Her father has set her curfew at 11:00 p.m. on Friday and Saturday nights. He has informed her that if she is not going to be in the house by eleven, she should call him at home and tell him where she is. He is clear that he wants her to call, not text or message otherwise. Michelle loves her father but finds the curfew restrictive. There have been nights when she did not arrive home at eleven and did not call. Sometimes she would text, but often she would not communicate at all, just arrive home late. She was with her friends and they were not up to any trouble. Since her friends were allowed to stay out later, she was self-conscious about her father expecting her to be home so "early"; what would her friends think? She would just wait a while longer, but not too late, so she wouldn't get in too much trouble. She would be home by eleven thirty or midnight. But she would not call her father to tell him. She assumed that if she did call, he would just be angry with her, so why bother?[23] Why couldn't he just trust her and know she is fine? When she did come home at eleven thirty or midnight, her father was upset with her actions—both coming home late and not calling. But he did not shout or anything. Rather, he expressed his disappointment, repeated the expectation, and they both went to bed. The first couple of times this happened, she figured that she did not get off too badly.

We can see here that Michelle does not recognize her father's perspective as different from her own. Instead, she presumes his concerns are what she imagines them to be: for her safety (likely); a desire to be punitive (not likely); and intent on ruining her fun (not likely). Furthermore, she thinks he is demanding, old fashioned, and even irrational. For one thing, her friends did not have the same curfew. For another, she prefers texting to a phone call because she can better avoid any "drama" coming from him. Finally, he should trust her! The fact that she brings "trust" into the equation indicates a new ability to imagine themes like trust. But the way she uses it shows she does not really understand how it works; she presumes that trust is established simply because she says so: "He should think me trustworthy because *I* think I am." So far, Michelle cannot see beyond her own self-interest. What will it take for her to begin to see her father's perspective? Different things could trigger it, but we return to this question later.

As well as a lack of appreciation for her father's perspective, Michelle is also still limited in her ability to connect consequences beyond immediate repercussions; because her father does not get too angry when she comes in a bit late, she thinks she has gotten off easy. However, when she asks permission to go away to a nearby city for a big concert with these same friends, her father says no, pointing to the fact that he cannot trust her to come home on time or even to call. Of course, to Michelle this response seems unreasonable; for her the two events are not connected. She promises that she will do whatever he wants if only she is permitted to go. She does not recognize that her failure to be reliable in the past has directly impacted her father's ability to trust her now. For him, the connection is very clear. For her, the denial of the concert request and his explanation makes this connection visible for the first time.

The ability to see and take on her father's perspective and the ability to develop a sense of long-term cause and effect are central to cross-categorical (third-order) knowing, according to Kegan. He notes that such knowing can take a variety of concrete categories (Michelle's behavior vis-à-vis her father on Friday nights) and thematize them (trust, consideration, and responsibility):

> The capacity to subordinate durable categories to the inter-action between them makes their thinking abstract, their feelings a matter of inner states and self-reflective emotion ("self-confident," "guilty," "depressed"), and their social-relating capable of loyalty and devotion to a community of people or ideas larger than the self.[24]

As well as ideation, cross-categorical knowing calls into use the capacities to think historically (behaviors over the past few months will impact decisions in future months). Both ideation and historical thinking are made possible and enhanced by the development and use of the frontal cortex. Cross-categorical knowing also calls for greater facility across the hemispheres of the brain, connecting areas of knowledge to serve larger ideas (e.g., linking emotions, desires, actions, consequence, and shifting perspectives). Thus the capacity to develop this kind of awareness and cognition necessary to recognize relationships and their contextual expectations is only first possible in adolescence. Furthermore, the facility to think cross-categorically, once begun, takes several years to develop, expand, and refine. At first it may appear haltingly or clumsily, with limited ability to recognize and act on what is seen. Kegan argues that there is often a gap between what adults expect of adolescent reasoning ability and what adolescents can do.[25]

Conclusion

This gap between what the adolescent recognizes and what is expected by others can remain a source of frustration or become a prompt for change. How well the adolescent bridges that gap may be determined by the support and challenge offered by those around her. In the next chapter, we continue examining what is meant by support and challenge and describe how relationships can trigger the transformation. We then consider a theological perspective, articulating how this is the work of God's grace.

7

Learning to Serve as Crew

With the move from a small, single-sail boat to a sloop comes the need for an additional sailor, as the sloop is most efficient when sailed with at least two crew members. The larger the boat, the more crew needed. Sailing with others changes the nature of sailing because coordination among sailors is required. Suddenly, each must communicate with the other and contribute together to the advancement of the boat. Learning to work in coordination with and consideration of others is an expectation of adulthood, whether at work, in school, on a team, or in a family. Learning this is an essential task of adolescence.

The development of the brain may make it possible to ideate and make sense in new ways, but it does not mean an adolescent will automatically see and respond to the world relationally. For example, the adolescent may begin to recognize things he has not seen before, but he will attribute a meaning that comes from his perspective, not from others. When someone responds negatively to his behavior, he will assume that they are having a bad day or that they do not like him. If *he* thinks his behavior was appropriate, he assumes that others will think so too. For him to learn otherwise will require him to shift his attention away from himself and pay attention long enough to the other so that he comes to understand their perspective. In fact, in chapter 5, we argued that it is the presence of the robust relationships in a young person's life—calling him to live into the relationships—that may push the young person to recognize the relationships and all they entail. For the robust relationship will call him to shift his attention beyond himself. To illustrate, let us return to the example initiated in chapter 6.

Relationships Trigger the Recognition of Relationships

Michelle notices that her father is still up when she gets home and goes to bed soon after she arrives, but at first, she does not think anything of it; her father usually stays up to watch the late news. One night, finally, she asks him why he is up when the news was over and the television off. He explains he was waiting for her to get home and that it is important that he see her when she comes in. As obvious as that may seem, it had never occurred to her. For the first time, she realizes that by staying out late, she has been keeping him up. She did not make that connection on her own. Rather, she assumed he was still awake because he wanted to stay up, just like she is doing what she wants by staying out past her curfew. She is only just beginning to see his perspective as different from what she imagined. Furthermore, she begins to see that her actions are impacting his actions; he does not wish to be up that late, but because of his care for her, he is. She begins to recognize her responsibility for his staying up. Because she cares for him, this becomes one more thing that causes Michelle to rethink staying out beyond her curfew. This shift is significant; she rethinks her actions not out of concern for punishment, but for how her they impact her father. It is the significance of Michelle's relationship with her father that helps her begin to see both the relationship between the two of them and its contextual expectations. Because he is not easily dismissed as irrelevant to her life, she is drawn to take his perspective into account.

Developmental theorist Robert Kegan, along with educational theorist Jack Mezirow, describes this kind of learning—removing oneself from one's perspective to see another's—as transformational.[1] It is not simply the learning of additional information, but a change in how that information is seen and ordered. Michelle moves from being embedded in her own perspective to becoming removed from it sufficiently to examine it side by side with her father's perspective. Not only is it new information (his perspective), but she transforms how she sees it (side by side with her own). Mezirow argues that, for transformation of this nature to happen, there needs to be a "disorienting dilemma" to initiate the shift.[2] A disorienting dilemma creates dissatisfaction within the young person's way of seeing and thinking such that it prompts her to remove herself from it. She begins to remove herself from, what Mezirow calls, one "meaning perspective" toward a wider, more expansive "meaning perspective."[3] In this case, it is the move for Michelle from the relatively narrow perspective of seeing her father as a fixed object around whom she has to maneuver to get what she wants (Kegan's *second order*), to the wider perspective in which "what she wants" is seen within the context of her relationship with her father, who has interests of his own (Kegan's *third order*).[4] The disorienting dilemma for this shift from second to third order for most adolescents can be a combination of internal and external factors. The internal factors are changes in the body, particularly the brain's ability to be self-conscious and reflective, noticing things previously invisible. The external factors are the shifting expectations of those around the young person. Because Michelle is getting older, she has a later curfew than she did as a younger child, but her father is expecting more of her now than he would have when she was younger.

However, disorientation on its own does not produce growth, it simply triggers the possibility. Kegan writes that "people grow best where they continuously experience an ingenious blend of support and challenge."[5] Kegan continues, "Such supports constitute a holding environment…a tricky transitional culture, an evolutionary bridge, a context for crossing over. It fosters developmental transformation, or the process by which the whole ('how I am') becomes gradually a part ('how I was') of a new whole ('how I am now')."[6]

If, on the one hand, the adolescent feels the expectations but cannot see what is being asked and why, then the situation is only supplying the challenge. For her, the result is likely to be frustration, anxiety, or anger triggered by this disconnect between what everyone seems to want of her and what she understands.[7] If, on the other hand, all impediments are removed from the adolescent's path, then the situation is only offering support. In this instance, the result may be her future inability to recognize and respond to expectations on her own.[8] It is in the context of our relationships that we experience the stress of expectations, but it is also in the context of relationships that we can begin to see the relationship as such, make sense of its demands, and learn to respond accordingly. Again, because this is a challenging set of tasks, it does not happen automatically. Rather, I suggest it is most likely to happen in specific robust relationships where there is *transparency* in meaning and purpose, sufficient *time*, and the presence of *care or respect*, like Michelle's relationship with her father. Let's now consider each of these.

TRANSPARENCY

Important signals within relationships can remain invisible or insignificant until we learn otherwise. Before I learned to sail, I had no way of knowing that the surface of the water could tell me about the movement of the air above the surface or the current below. While noticeable, the surface remained meaningless. One afternoon, during that first summer of lessons, the wind died, and our boat was sitting still in the water. Afraid we were stuck there, I asked our instructor if we should pull out the paddles. She said no and pointed across the water to indicate a change in the water's surface. "The wind is coming; it will be here soon, and we will be on our way." She was right. I could see the small ripples moving across the water toward us, and then I could feel the slight breeze on my skin and see it fill the sails; indeed, we were soon moving along. Her instruction helped me look to the surface of the water for changes in wind or current speed, but I am still not very good at it. I still need help from more experienced sailors and expect to get better with practice.

Similarly, relationships are full of subtle shifts and movements. Recognizing the signals and interpreting them accurately takes years of instruction and practice. As in sailing, some of the most meaningful instruction is not from instructional manuals or classrooms "on the hard."[9] Rather, the best learning happens "on the water," within the course of real relationships. For there we come to recognize the signs in context and feel the subtle or not-so-subtle shifts as they happen. If in real relationships, in real time, adults articulate and make more visible what is expected and why, the adolescent is more likely to come to recognize what was previously invisible and respond to it. In Michelle's case, appreciation for her father's perspective came through conversations wherein her father explained himself: "I'm up when you get home because I'm waiting for you." He could also take other occasions to explain why he wants her home by eleven o'clock and why he wants her to call if she expects she will be late: "I want you safely at home; you need your sleep; and things are likely to get more problematic the later it gets, no matter who is involved. I want a phone call rather than a text because I want to hear your voice and I want you to hear mine; there's less of a chance to hide in a phone call. If you do call to say you will be late, I am going to ask where you are, who you are with, when you plan to get home, and how you plan to get home. I am soberly waiting to determine whether you are sober when you return. I need to know these things to help ensure your safety. I am not only considering your behavior, but also all the others whom you might meet while out late." Left to depend on her perspective, Michelle will attribute her own rationale to his behavior. It takes him, or some other reliable source, to make transparent what she cannot see and know on her own. As she learns his perspective, she comes to know what he thinks about her being out late with friends, but she will also begin to imagine how he thinks about other situations.

As adolescents gain the capacity to ideate and interpret, reasons and reasoning take on far more value than was possible in childhood. The old line "Because I said so!" has less and less sway than it did earlier. As mentioned in chapter 6, the growing brain can recognize signs, connect ideas, and connect cause and effect, but these connections must be made obvious and repeatedly for the adolescent's interpretative capacity to become accurate and fluid. Unfortunately, parents and other adults may be more frustrated by conversation at this point in their relationships. In part, it is because adolescents find the exchanges challenging; the new efforts in thinking are hard and most do not want to appear inept. In fact, adolescent psychologist David Elkind notes that what he calls adolescent argumentativeness is in fact a necessary developmental skill whereby they practice making sense of the new world of ideas. For their own part, adults may find the need for repetition and explanation intellectually and emotionally exhausting.[10] To diffuse the possibility for overly emotional exchanges, Elkind recommends that adults steer the discussions toward concepts, like principles and values, and try not to get caught up in issues of taste or preference unless connected to a larger concept.[11] This helps the adolescent to interpret accurately and respond appropriately. During adolescence, talking—articulating ideas and reasons—becomes more important than ever before, even as it becomes more challenging.

However, this does not mean that parents should do all the thinking for their son or daughter. Many parents may feel it is easier—less prone to failure and less stressful—if they make decisions or do things for their son or daughter rather than shepherd them through the messy process. Such parents may hope that their children learn from their example. In part, such learning can happen. But if the son or daughter is not allowed multiple opportunities to work things out on his or her own, he or she may infer all sorts of unintended messages: that they are not capable; that everything must be done perfectly on the first attempt; that mistakes are intolerable.[12] Just as parents learn to guide a toddler's first steps, offering safety and support followed by greater freedom to roam unsupported, so too parents need to provide similar incremental guidance and freedom for the new cognitive capacities gained through adolescence. The adolescent learns from trial and error, taking risks and making mistakes, as well as taking responsibility and recovering from mistakes made. Such learning is not done in a vacuum, but within increasingly widening parameters of guidance and support.

TIME

It takes time for things to become transparent to the growing adolescent, for such naming and recognizing is not a one-time event. It should happen in many and diverse ways, but with patience and a consistency of message. Anyone who has worked with adolescents will be familiar with the need to explain and explain and explain again, until the moment when suddenly the adolescent sees what you are talking about. Until then, your words appear as mindless blather. The irony is that after they do recognize and understand, many adolescents wonder why you did not tell them sooner and frequently accuse you of holding back necessary information! The fact is they could not see until they could see, and seeing makes all the difference. Mezirow notes that once that first recognition happens and the wider frame of reference begins to emerge, details fall into place.[13] Now, Michelle's father may have explained his reasoning to her in the past. But it is not until she lives into them, does so consistently, and sees how he responds that she comes to appreciate and understand what he means. The challenging—and often frustrating—thing for both Michelle and her father is that learning like this is not a one-and-done experience, but takes time and repetition. The grace for Michelle in this situation is that her relationship with her father is long term and touches so many aspects of her life. He has many different opportunities to communicate with her. Furthermore, we see him investing in the relationship and favoring nonmediated communication so that the subtleties of the relationship can be noticed and used. Such a relationship is more likely to be conducive to repeatedly and consistently communicating important lessons.

Time also allows Michelle to recognize other relational dynamics. For example, she learns that *trustworthiness*, or truthfulness, is not just a word she can claim to suit her purposes. Rather, it is a value that is determined—or not—based on a person's consistent behavior. As frustrating as it may be for her, it is her father who will determine when she is trustworthy. In time, she will appreciate that her consistent displays of reliability are how she can build up that trust. Also, in time, she may come to appreciate and take on the same relational values as her father. Michelle may benefit further as she transfers these values to other relationships, figuring out how to trust others and build trust with them. Time within a specific relationship grants Michelle the space to recognize what she did not see before, make sense of it anew, see how it plays out within that relationship, and potentially transfer it to other relationships.

Finally, time spent within the relationship with her father helps her learn long-term cause and effect. It is a big move from the simple tit-for-tat reciprocity that children can see to the ability to appreciate the long-term consequences that may take months or years to spin out. Likewise, it takes time to recognize that actions in one sphere or relationship (e.g., poor performance for a first employer) may have implications in another (e.g., later inability to get a good reference). Since it takes so much time to recognize these connections and consequences, it is helpful for the early adolescent to start taking on reasonable responsibility for her actions as soon as possible, for larger responsibilities will pile up unbidden as she moves into later adolescence and early adulthood.

CARE AND RESPECT

Given that the adolescent encounters so many people in his life, which ones will prompt the change to a relational perspective? Those close relationships in which he has developed a sense of attachment, like parents, are likely contexts for him to learn.[14] But given the proclivity to misattribute adult intention, it should not be assumed that he will recognize his parents' love as unconditional and specific to him. Amid the self-consciousness of adolescence, he may suddenly question if anyone really loves him for himself. He will scan the world for some validation, including the potentially thousands of connections that are digitally mediated. But very few of them will be relationships of care and respect, and many of them will be completely anonymous. With adolescence, it becomes important that other adults, alongside parents, step forward and affirm his value to him. In response to the experience of care and respect, there is a greater likelihood he will listen to what is shared by the adult. He is less likely to dismiss the demands and instructions of those others who do not dismiss him.

Navigating relationships successfully calls us into observing, interpreting, and mastering a multitude of subtleties, and no one person is an expert. Rather, we can learn from multiple sources. In my second summer of sailing, when I joined the Thursday racing group and crewed for different skippers,[15] I found that no two skippers sailed the same. In fact, they even gave the same directions a bit differently. So while I was able to transfer my growing set of skills from one boat to the next, I still had to pay attention to how each skipper wanted me to accomplish those tasks. While at times I was frustrated by what seemed confusing or contrary, in time I learned to value what each offered and recognized patterns under the diversity of directions. They each expanded my repertoire of skills as crew member and my ability to finesse as situations demanded.

Similarly, adolescents benefit from having significant robust relationships with multiple adults. Throughout this section, I have focused on Michelle and her father, and while the parental relationship is usually the most consistent in a young person's life, it is not the only one that can communicate these lessons. In fact, the relationship between parent and child can be so loaded with emotions and expectations that it is sometimes not the best relationship for a growing adolescent to begin to find their own voice and sense of direction. If an adolescent has a significant, long-term relationship with at least one other mature adult, it increases the possibility that someone is helping them see and connect the dots. Those adults may be teachers, coaches, or other paid professionals, but I highlight the importance of others whom we often overlook: aunts and uncles, grandparents, neighbors, congregation members, parents of friends, and friends of parents. It is helpful for adolescents to be surrounded by adults who are simply living their adult lives and who offer adolescents some transparency in what that demands, the benefit of time over months and years, and the opportunity for care and respect to grow and be communicated in the relationship.

The Transforming Spirit

Beyond the neurobiological and cognitive developmental framework, theological claims are also appropriate for this discussion. The first claim, which was initially proposed in chapter 3, is that we are always in relationship with God simply because God has created us in and for relationships. Therefore, the relational transformation is not *bringing* the adolescent into relationship with God, for that relationship, as *uncreated grace*, precedes everything.[16] Through the gift of *created grace*, the adolescent can be transformed; he can become aware of the relationship, and so by being aware, participate in it more fully, more consciously and constructively. Thus, from a ministerial perspective, there is value in assisting the adolescent to gain this relational capacity so that he may be more able to live into the call of Christian discipleship. The second claim is that transformative grace is the gift of the Holy Spirit, from whom all life and all holiness come. I close this chapter by naming how the Holy Spirit is present and active within the adolescent and his robust relationships to help him see himself in relationship with God and with the world. To repeat, it is essential for an adolescent to know himself to be valued for himself. As he experiences himself as loved, he very naturally turns in generosity to love others. Love, both received and expressed, is the medium in which his relational capacity grows. It creates the opportunity to discover his unique personhood and acknowledge the personhood of another.

RECEIVING MYSELF AS GIFT

In a renewed theology of vocation, Edward Hahnenberg turns to Jesuit theologian Karl Rahner to describe how God's call is personal to the individual. "Sharing the confidence of Ignatius of Loyola, Rahner believed that it is natural for God to reveal God's will to individuals." Hahnenberg continues that this revelation is not "spelled out in the clouds…[but] is more like a 'sense' or an 'awareness' of something that is both within and beyond us. Rahner called this 'sense' of ourselves and of God 'transcendental experience.'"[17] The awareness Rahner describes requires a capacity for self-consciousness; not only the ability for the individual to have an inner life, but to see himself seeing it. Self-consciousness enables him to see himself located within a horizon—amid a reality bigger than and beyond him. It creates the opportunity for the adolescent to recognize that there is more to life and more to him than meets the eye. Somehow he is "on stage," seen by others, and that stage and their seeing means something, even as he is unsure what.[18] It is because of this capacity that questions of identity arise: who am I and where do I fit in? While such questions may seem simply social, they are deeply existential; for the new awareness of the greater horizon introduces the possibility of being lost or insignificant. In fact, through the growth in self-consciousness, God awakens in the adolescent the potential for a new awareness of himself as human but also a new awareness of God as the horizon on which he sees himself. This awareness is beyond and different from an instrumental understanding of God, who takes care of what is needed, but otherwise is not demanding or involved with life—what Christian Smith names as *moralistic therapeutic deism*.[19] Through the adolescent's growth, God creates the possibility for upsetting the adolescent's prior conceptions of God and creating a new relational dynamic between himself and God.

Hahnenberg explains that "for Rahner, that infinite horizon of the human person is nothing less than the mystery of God….God is the horizon that opens up the landscape and encircles our lives, calling us forward even as it continually recedes before us."[20] Hahnenberg goes on to write,

> We cannot "know" the mystery of God in the same way we know ordinary objects. And yet—in a move central to his theological project—Rahner argued that this horizon can be "known" in another way: not through an explicit, categorical delineation but through an implicit, preconceptual awareness. We have a "sense," a "consciousness," of our infinite openness to God and of God's gracious presence to us.[21]

Hahnenberg writes, "The experience of God is something we all share—a sense of silent mystery swirling within and around us."[22] Therefore, the growth of self-consciousness provides the opportunity to "grow more conscious of this transcendent presence within ourselves, to sink more deeply into it…[and so] come to understand ourselves more fully."[23] The adolescent comes to see himself on a wider horizon; he may name that wider horizon as God, or at least name God as another being on the horizon with whom he can now be in relationship.[24] Either way, he may enter into a relational understanding of God.

We cannot presume that the adolescent is automatically going to think to name these experiences of transcendence—this sense of a wider horizon—as an experience of God. The experiences may prompt the adolescent to imagine that there is more to life than was previously conceived, but to name this experience of the transcendent as the love of God is far from automatic. While the experiences may offer moments of well-being, it can also provoke a threatening sense of vastness that renders the adolescent invisible or insignificant.[25] In order for the adolescent to name the experience as love, he needs someone offering the language and experience of love. Hahnenberg points to the need for a community and narrative: "I only recognize such experience as the experience of God because I have been shaped within a context in which the experience of God is meaningful."[26] The adolescent needs a wise guide to help interpret their experience, just as the priest Eli helps Samuel, who "did not yet know the LORD," to recognize that it is the Lord calling (see 1 Sam 3:1–10).

To internalize this understanding, the adolescent needs transparency, time, and care. Someone must articulate the story of God's love for the adolescent to see it as such. But that love only becomes believable when the adolescent experiences being loved. The experience of being loved by another human person creates the possibility that the adolescent will perceive himself as valuable in God's eyes and recognize God's horizon as a secure environment in which he is carefully held. Hahnenberg writes, "What saves us is a friendship. God offers God's self to us in love, and invites us to respond in kind."[27] For God's love to be recognized and believed as such, it needs to be articulated and felt in real persons, who embody God's love.

RECOGNIZING THE GIFT OF THE OTHER

While the love of God serves the individual, it is not self-serving. At the heart of the Christian story is a paradox: to save your life, you must lose it (see Luke 9:24). Concerning adolescent transformation, this paradox comes to life: for an adolescent to be transformed into someone who can see and engage in the world relationally, she must risk the vulnerable work of loving and being loved; she must go out to meet the other and allow the other to meet her. The adolescent does not need inert mirrors, reflecting her projections; rather, she needs real people to reflect back to her the real person they see and to present their real selves in the process, so that she may see her impact on them and acknowledge theirs on her.

In his own work, Hahnenberg suggests the postmodern experience of plurality—the experience of otherness—may be the most challenging mark of the age. However, he argues that the encounter with the other can reveal the encounter with God. I suggest that anyone who recognizes the adolescent, takes her seriously, and calls her to recognize them in kind serves as the "other" for the adolescent. They may not be too distant or too different; it may be a close friend, sibling, or a parent. But this other is no longer simply an extension of herself, nor simply an instrument in her life, but someone with a life and story of their own that sets them apart from her. Hahnenberg writes, "To acknowledge difference brings with it a demand to let the other stand. We cannot absorb all other narratives into our own."[28] For the first time, the other's story is heard, interrupting her self-concept, such that she needs to retell her own story so as to account for them in her life.

Hahnenberg looks to theologian Lieven Boeve, who, drawing from Matthew 25:40, calls us to see Jesus revealed in our attention to the other. According to Hahnenberg, Boeve "uses the language of *interruption* to name this encounter with 'the other.'"[29] For Boeve, "an interruption cuts into a story already being told....Thus the interruption is not destructive. It is transformative—if we are open to it. Our stories go on, but they go on changed."[30] Hahnenberg continues the line of thought: "In the face of these interruptions—global and personal, negative and positive—we are called through ourselves and our experiences, through others and their very different experiences, toward *the* Other, who also always escapes our grasp."[31]

In just this way, the adolescent is surprised by the demands of family and friends such that she needs to take them seriously. They interrupt her story in which she was the center of the world. Now her story becomes one in which she is in relationship with those she holds dear. Hahnenberg goes on to explain how these experiences of the other are an experience of God:

God interrupts—God calls to us—when that silent mystery that always pulses beneath our lives bubbles up or bursts forth in our experience of encounter with the other....The Spirit works in and through the other to shake us out of our closed and self-assured stories, awakening us to a mystery deeper than any of our group projects or individual plans.[32]

Thus the encounter and interruption of the other creates a graced moment of transformation. Such interruptions happen for the adolescent when she opens herself to a new awareness and attentiveness to the others in her life. Her presumptions about the other are replaced with a deeper, more accurate understanding, calling her to see them for who they are.[33]

This transformation is the work of the Holy Spirit, growing, prompting, encouraging, and inviting her to see herself and her world. But the presence of the Spirit within her must be met by the presence of the Spirit in the other. As she looks out to her world with her new capacity to see, the loving response of the other affirms her in herself and calls her out to the other. Her life becomes a valuable gift, which she is inspired to give to others.

Conclusion

Adolescence is an amazing moment in the human life span. Because of the plasticity of the adolescent brain and the expanding social world of the adolescent, this is a tremendous moment of opportunity for growth. She becomes able to see the world with more complexity and engage in the world with greater agency and nuance than was possible when she was a child. And the world expects her to do so. Of value is her development of self-consciousness that makes possible the movement beyond an instrumental worldview to a relational perspective. The ability to see the links between herself and others, between cause and effect, between agency and consequence, initiate a new appreciation in the adolescent of her own life and her relationship with the world. She comes to recognize that there is something unique about her—she is someone—and that she stands amid a wide world that is looking back at her. Rather than an inevitable shift that happens with the progress of time, this transformation is composed of multiple, interrelated tasks that can be learned and accomplished — or not. Robust relationships with others who cannot be ignored provide the curriculum, the classroom, and the inspiration for learning these tasks. In this rather extended moment — for it will take years — she may come to see that she is someone and that her life has consequence for others, and she begins to live into that new sense of herself in relation to the world.

Part Four
A DIVERSE FLEET

The church as an ark is an ancient image. Like Noah's ark (Gen 6:14–22), it is a means of salvation and sometimes referred to as the Barque of Peter. The image is reflected in church architecture; the word *nave*, the body of the church building, is drawn from the Latin *navis*, for ship. More recently, however, the image of the church as ark might bring to mind a modern cruise ship, wherein the church members are passengers served by the ordained leadership. Like vacationers lured by the promise of endless buffets and entertainment, congregants have become consumers of church services rather than contributors to its movement. However, cruises have their limitations. It is easy to get lost on a cruise ship amid the thousands of passengers. A cruise ship is not nimble; its destinations are limited to those ports deep enough to handle the ship. Its itinerary does not reflect the gifts of its passengers, who remain inert recipients of services.

What if we imagine the church as a diverse fleet? Composed of vessels of all sizes and designs, each is fully functioning and able to reach diverse waters. Sometimes boats work in tandem, whether on open sea, small inlets, rivers, bayous, or bays. Each serves as an instantiation of the church's presence and effort; each boat drawing on the contributions of its crew members—whether two or fifty-two. Each one serves as a place of apprenticeship, sharing the stories and practices of sailing. Imagining the church in this way, it is easy to recognize how nimble and diversely present the church is in the world.

Likewise, we can see how younger members are brought into the life and work of the church. Finally, like the skills of sailing, those of discipleship in Christ are highly transferable. While the disciple's community may change, he will be able to contribute reliably to the practices and narratives in the new setting.

In this final part of the book, we turn our attention from the individual adolescent to the ecclesial community surrounding the adolescent. We identify the kind of church that appropriately companions the adolescent to maturity. The ecclesial community—as parishes, dioceses, secondary schools, or higher educational settings, but also families, small faith communities, social networks, and service agencies—might intentionally provide a community of robust relationships that invite adolescents to imagine their lives on the horizon of God's infinite love. Those relationships within the community can help adolescents recognize that their primary relationship is with God and that it precedes all others and makes all possible. The community does this by inviting adolescents to interpret their lives in light of that relationship. Yet this is not accomplished through a particular program or strategy, but by inviting each adolescent to join in the life of the community, which itself is proclaiming, attending, interpreting, celebrating, and acting on that same belief. The narratives of God's infinite love are made credible and compelling to adolescents when embodied in loving relationships with real people, a communion of saints present to the adolescent.

The church is neither a community for its members' entertainment nor a place of disconnected obligations. Rather, it is a community with narratives and practices that support a mission for the life in community and for the life of the world. In chapter 8, we examine how the narratives of the community provide a horizon upon which the adolescent might imagine his life. In the ninth chapter, we consider how the practices within the community apprentice the adolescent to maturing membership and interpretation.

8

Sharing a Storied Horizon

In sailboat racing there is a distinction made between strategy and tactics. Strategy is the plan for the race that you make just prior, which factors in conditions on the course. It requires you to look out across the water to note things like which side of the course has more wind, where the current is the strongest, and which end of the starting line is favored. These considerations play into a strategy for sailing the race. One of the advantages an experienced racer has over a novice is making that prerace strategy. However, during the race, the location and movement of other sailboats impact that strategy. So within the race you practice tactics that help you keep to your strategy or adapt appropriately. The tactics may give you an advantage over other boats or put other boats at a disadvantage. For example, you might change the course of your boat to keep in clear air and out of the wind shadow of another boat; that would be an advantaging tactic. If that same move also created a wind shadow for a different downwind boat, the tactic would create a disadvantage for that other boat. Sometimes in the heat of the race a clever tactic can appear very compelling, even if it draws you away from the ultimate strategy of doing well in the race. An experienced racer is less likely to be drawn into the clever tactic, knowing it ultimately will not pay off. Being able to judge the value of short-term gains against long-term goals is a capacity that comes with practice and reflection. It requires assessing the race after the fact, being honest when things do not work, and amending your practice.

Throughout the book we have argued that the adolescent's central project is to find her place in the world. It involves tasks of self-seeing, seeing the other, and recognizing the relationship between. It is foremost an interpretive task for the adolescent as she figures out her world so that she can figure out her place in it. All these tasks are interrelated; each calls the adolescent to decenter from a prior conception of her place in the world to one wherein she is in relation to others. These tasks draw her from the short-term, immediate self-interest of childish thinking to the long-term, relational considerations expected of mature adults. In a sense, this growth is akin to developing the ability to strategize—to plan along a horizon—as well as act tactfully in the moment in service to that strategy. However, unlike a sailing race, the strategic goal of adulthood is not to win a competition; rather, it is to live responsibility within the context of relationships.

This concept of adulthood is grounded in the Christian narrative of the triune God and the life, death, and resurrection of Jesus. The horizon of God's love is the course upon which we invite the adolescent to strategize her life. Theologian Catherine LaCugna argues that just as Christians conceive of God as a Trinity of persons-in-relation, so too, human persons are made to be in relationships of responsible and generous love, mutuality, and justice. LaCugna writes, "Persons are by definition indefinable, unique, ineffable. To say that someone is a person is to acknowledge that we cannot exactly and completely define him or her."[1] The Christian narrative holds that to live in love is to recognize the dignity and value of each person. To do so is not counterproductive to human life or the way the world works. Rather, it is to participate with the grace of God already acting within each person and within the world. This narrative provides the larger strategy. The infinite love of God *is* the horizon upon which all lives are lived such that each life is recognized as uniquely valuable. As the adolescent matures toward adulthood, she is called to see her life as a unique and valuable gift of God, and she is to grow continually in openness to the other so as to recognize their life as uniquely valuable.

To interpret her life and the world, as such, she needs to become familiar with the Christian narratives that provide this horizon. Robust relationships serve as an important setting in which these narratives are learned. They are where the adolescent experiences being loved and is called to love. Furthermore, they are the setting wherein the adolescent is drawn deeply into the narratives and practices of the Christian community that help her develop the strategy for her life. Through narration amid robust relationships within the communion of saints, she will come to see her life in light of the love of God.

Looking to the Horizon

A robust relationship between an adolescent and an adult can provide the imaginative horizon upon which the adolescent might interpret his life. In chapter 1, we considered the philosopher Hans-Georg Gadamer, who wrote,

> The horizon is the range of vision that includes everything that can be seen from a particular vantage point....A person who has no horizon does not see far enough and hence overvalues what is nearest to him. On the other hand, "to have a horizon" means not being limited to what is nearby but being able to see beyond it. A person who has a horizon knows the relative significance of everything within this horizon, whether it is near or far, great or small.[2]

As discussed in chapter 6, the adolescent is only just gaining the cognitive capacity to look beyond his immediate self-interest. A horizon invites him to look beyond himself and beyond the immediate such that he can imagine his life in an expansive way. Yet like the novice racer who needs to be encouraged to look beyond the immediate tactic to see the larger strategy, the adolescent needs to be encouraged, even trained, to look up from the immediate and to see far enough so that he does not, as Gadamer writes, "overvalue what is nearest to him."[3]

Research in adolescent development has shown that one of the most crucial factors for adolescents to develop a longer horizon, or a sense of purpose, is the presence and encouragement of adults who "provide affirmation, cultivation, and guidance."[4] These relationships enable the adolescent to develop a "sense of direction in committing to a purpose."[5] Robust relationships within the Christian community may provide these and can do so along a very particular Christian horizon. Theologian Edward Hahnenberg writes, "What grounds our knowing (as well as our choosing and our loving) is neither an unending emptiness nor absolute Being. It is the God of Jesus Christ. God is the horizon that opens up the landscape and encircles our lives, calling us forward even as it continually recedes before us."[6] Thus the Christian community offers the adolescent the promise of God's infinite love and belief that we are made to live in relationships of love as the horizon on which to imagine his life. And through the communion of saints, the Christian community provides examples of lives interpreted along that horizon.

Since this horizon stands in dramatic contrast to dominant cultural narratives of individual pursuit and private advantage, it may defy belief, particularly for an adolescent who does not recognize love in his own life. The horizon of God's infinite love is made more accessible and credible within the closer horizon of a robust relationship whereby the adolescent experiences himself as loved. Love becomes believable in the felt experience of being loved. The value of this loving relationship with a more mature adult cannot be underestimated for affirming the value of the individual. Furthermore, the more immediate horizon of a robust relationship provides the space wherein the adolescent can learn of his unique agency, consequence, and value, and thus provides a horizon and a narrative by which the adolescent can come to imagine his life beyond that relationship. The robust relationship creates the arena wherein the life of the individual adolescent may come into conversation with the incredible stories of faith and grace. As a result, those stories become *our* stories—powerful, credible, and inspiring.

The Loss of Stories

Stories are what constitute communities and hold them together. Stories offer direction, history, and purpose. It may seem ironic, however, to propose stories just when adolescents claim to "see through" our stories. By late childhood, they have already questioned the stories of Santa Claus and the Easter Bunny. And by early adolescence, as they learn of the big bang theory and evolution, they dismiss the story of the world being created by God in six days. By late adolescence, they also question the various miracle accounts they hear, and wonder about a God who did great, dramatic things in the past but now seems so quiet. Or they reconsider miracles and healing stories, questioning a

God who chooses to heal some and not others. Such actions on God's part begin to seem capricious and arbitrary, and perhaps not worthy of their belief. Likewise, they see an ecclesial community that does not always practice the mercy, justice, and love it preaches. With the capacity to see and make sense of the observable "facts" of this world, religious stories and beliefs, which seem to defy those facts, lose their credibility as the young person matures.

According to developmental theorist James Fowler, such incredulity marks the adolescent move beyond the *mythic-literal* faith that is characteristic of later childhood. Mythic-literal faith, by which the older child can hear and narrate stories, enables her to generate stories of her own, allowing her to "conserve, communicate, and compare their experiences and meanings."[7] Likewise, the older child can "construct God's perspective, giving it as much richness—and some of the same limits—as the perspectives now consistently attributed to friends and family."[8] However, these same stories create the boundaries of meaning; the child is not yet able to step outside of those stories to read the intention or deeper meaning within them. In fact, for the child, Fowler writes, "Presumably God created this ordering of things and even God is bound to the lawfulness that he has created."[9] However, the mythic-literal stage begins to break down when the growing child gains the mental capacities to ideate and think thematically. She discovers that these stories of faith conflict with the laws of nature, or she finds that God's actions defy a sense of fairness. Fowler writes of the "'eleven-year-old atheists'...[who] begin to experience the breakdown of the moral principle of reciprocity they have used to compose their images of God. By observation and experience, they have found that either God is powerless...[or] 'asleep.'"[10] As the growing adolescent comes to see the world with greater complexity, she is disappointed in a God who does not seem to be up to the task, and so leaves this God behind as unreliable or unhelpful.

Many adults become disheartened by the adolescent's loss of credulity. In response, they may try to make such stories believable by manipulating the factual framework (e.g., "Perhaps the seven days were not twenty-four-hour days; maybe they were longer.") or arguing that you simply have to believe because that is what it means to have faith. Too often we try to push adolescents—and ourselves—into a simplistic and literal reading of religious stories, knowing we are doomed from the start. Consequently, we do a disservice to adolescents, ourselves, and the religious narratives. Adolescents would be better served by adults admitting that they too find many religious stories—whether biblical or hagiographic—inadequate as historic or scientific fact.[11] Without these conversations, the "eleven-year-old atheist" ages into the twentysomething atheist, or at the very least, someone inarticulately holding a deeply inadequate conception of God.[12]

The Retrieval of Stories

This loss of stories calls for a novel approach. When we stop fighting for their factual believability, we open the opportunity to investigate their theological value. For example, when we stop arguing that the Creation accounts found in the bible are valuable as historic or scientific explanations of the beginning of the world, we can begin to explore them for their *theological value*. We can explore them for what they claim about God, about the relationship of God to all creation, and about our relationship to God and to the rest of creation. We can move away from debating *how* the world came to be, and we can move toward proclaiming as Christians that we believe *that* the world came to be because God called/calls it into existence. Our claim is that life is; we believe that its ultimate source is God, and that God claims creation is good and very good (Gen 1).[13] To articulate it in such terms is to simultaneously recognize alternative possibilities (e.g., that there could be nothing) and interpretations (e.g., that creation is not in competition with itself as it comes from a sole source). By unpacking the theological sense of our stories, we open a world of possibility and enter more directly into a discussion on life's meaning, value, and direction. We invite the adolescent into an interpretive tradition that takes the biblical text seriously, to be surprised by the truth encountered therein. By shifting to a discussion on meaning, we move the religious discourse to an arena more appropriate and needed for a modern and postmodern world, and one needed by the adolescent growing toward adulthood.[14]

Fowler names this stage of faith as *synthetic-conventional*, whereby the adolescent becomes able to synthesize "stories, values, and beliefs into a supportive and orienting unity."[15] It is conventional in that the synthesis is drawn from what is "derived from one's significant others...

[even as it is]…formed into a novel, individual configuration."[16] While a young person may outgrow the stories and images of God that were previously satisfying, it is not automatic that she will take on the perspective of synthetic-conventional. Fowler's research indicates that "this involves a process of drawing together into an original unity a selection of the values, beliefs, and orienting convictions that are made available to the adolescent through her or his significant relationships and face-to-face interactions with others."[17] In other words, the adolescent needs the people around her to articulate these values and beliefs in a credible and compelling manner for her to assimilate them. The stories are then no longer fanciful and unbelievable stories that crumble in the face of real life. Instead, they become stories of meaning and value, unpacked for what they say about life, God, and who we are in the world. These become stories that ground the adolescent in the community of believers. This community invites the adolescent to interpret the world from the perspective of God's abiding presence and infinite love. The adolescent needs to hear these stories of God's action connected with the real lives of credible witnesses so that she might learn to make similar connections in her own life. Hahnenberg writes, "To be drawn into the narrative of Christ is what marks the first step on the path of discipleship. It is the necessary prerequisite to vocational discernment."[18] The deeper stories of the tradition, embodied and told in the lives of real people with whom she is in relationship, all help the adolescent train her imagination so that she might interpret her life along the horizon of God's infinite love.

Philosopher Alasdair MacIntyre claims that the human is "essentially a story-telling animal," by which he means that the human needs to make sense of her life and her actions, and does so through stories.[19] As the adolescent leaves behind childhood and moves toward adulthood, stories take on new value. They help her interpret the world in all the complexity she is newly recognizing, they shape her self-understanding, and they offer direction and purpose to her actions. However, as discussed in chapter 5, she does not compose her story out of thin air, but from the surrounding cultural narratives. The dominant cultural narratives tend to focus on individual rights and freedoms, privileging consumption and marketability. Within such narratives, her value is provisional, and her actions are determined by what is immediately expedient. For her to compose a meaningful story for her own life—grounded in the Christian narrative—she must know the Christian narrative to be meaningful. MacIntyre writes, "Deprive children of stories and you leave them unscripted, anxious stutters in their actions as in their words."[20] She needs bigger stories, worthy of her attention, to provide direction and purpose to her life and actions. When faced with adolescent incredulity, adult believers need to take the opportunity to unpack the meaning held within the Christian narrative, rather than force-feed the unbelievable. Likewise, the Christian community needs to intentionally invite the maturing adolescent into shaping the stories of who the community is.

Here again we can see the value of looking to the communion of saints. The Christian narrative is, in fact, many narratives, growing from the vast communion of saints across time and location. None of those stories are preordained or prescripted, but communicate that the individual's story borrows from, is contained within, and adds to the larger story of God's presence and action in the world. These lives find their meaning and direction in the life, death, and resurrection of Jesus. The communion of saints can be understood as an interpretive community in which each member has struggled over time to hear and respond to the word of God in his or her life. Like the saints, the adolescent is invited to interpret the mystery that is her own life and come to appreciate more deeply the mystery that is God. For her to receive her life as a gift given by God is the entry point of her salvation. As Hahnenberg writes, "God calls us forward to respond by carrying forward our deepest identity—to be saints by being ourselves."[21] The adolescent is compelled and companioned by the communion of saints to see and live into the saint within herself.

Narrating Our Lives onto a Horizon

As we have argued throughout, but especially in chapter 6, for the adolescent to grow from the self-interested perspective of childhood to the relational perspective needed in adulthood requires a transformational shift. More than an increase in capacity, it is an increase in complexity, whereby the adolescent must recognize that other people are no longer atomistic objects in his world but persons with whom he is in relationship. As Christians, we might also name this shift as a conversion, which Hahnenberg names as a move "from our attachments to a false sense of ourselves, our needs, and our plans" to a wider conception of who we are in relationship to others.[22] We understand that conversion is not a one-time event but a constant turning and turning again toward the more appropriate direction. Just as the wind and the current are constantly in flux and the sailor needs to adjust the boat to stay on the right course, so too are we constantly in flux, drawn this way and that and in need of constant *metanoia* (change of heart) so as to stay on course. By inviting an adolescent to see their lives within the narrative practices of the Christian life, we invite them to engage in narrative tactics by which the adolescent will find direction and stay on course. This goes well beyond the memorization of stories to include interpreting those stories in light of their life and vice versa.[23]

REVEALING A MEANINGFUL FRAMEWORK

MacIntyre argues that human action can only be properly understood in the context and intent of the action; in other words, within its historical narrative. He illustrates this, for example, by asking, when we see an older adolescent bent over a book, how do we know what he is doing? MacIntyre suggests that the answers could be varied: he is reading a book, studying for a biology exam, preparing to be a doctor, or hoping to be of aid to others. MacIntyre claims that we make the best sense of that young man's activity by knowing the wider story that surrounds the activity. By such an illustration, MacIntyre argues that actions in and of themselves do not tell us enough; they require a wider narrative to make sense. "We cannot…characterize behavior independently of intentions, and we cannot characterize intentions independently of the settings which make those intentions intelligible both to agents themselves and to others."[24] Therefore discovering the narrative frame is an essential tool for recognizing the meaning of an action.

Similarly, within robust relationships, narratives assist adolescents to move beyond the atomistic and self-interested consideration of their actions. Recall that for the child or young adolescent, functioning from within an instrumental perspective, actions are only right or wrong because some authority claimed them as so. However, if the act is advantageous to the adolescent, and she thinks she can get away with it, it is likely she will try to do so. Like Michelle in chapter 7, simply repeating the rules will likely have no impact. For her to gain the capacity to see herself as a moral agent—as a person whose choices matter

115

for the world—requires that she shift from the narrow perspective of immediate self-interest to a wider perspective. That requires someone else to share a narrative in which the action takes on meaning. For Michelle, it was her father being transparent about why he wanted her home at her curfew that caused her to see her actions within a wider frame of reference.

Narratives provide this wider context and intention. Beyond "because the church says so," the adolescent—and all adults, really—need the narrative to break open an explanation of *why* the church came to that teaching, what *values* it upholds, *how* it has developed over time, and *how* one lives life in light of it. Beyond the reasonableness of the church's argument, the robust relationship provides the context of a life in which the teaching is interpreted and made obvious. The adolescent also benefits from witnessing an adult believer struggling with tough questions; thus she sees that Christian faith is neither mindless assent nor ready-made. In response to which the adolescent may say, "If you believe and live this way, I can believe it and live it too." The belief needs to be framed within the story of real people's real lives.

Consider the young Francis of Assisi. In his wish to imitate Christ more closely, he renounced his wealth and took up a life of poverty. He attracted companions to the life of poverty, not because they blindly followed him, but because they were attracted to his interpretation of discipleship. Likewise, for the adolescent who is only beginning to recognize the links among acts, the narrative frame helps him interpret, value, and gain a sense of cause and effect that moves beyond the short term and immediately gratifying to develop a sense of consequence for his actions.

LEARNING TO ACT FOR THE GREATER GOOD

MacIntyre continues his illustration to show how knowledge of a goal (e.g., preparing to be a doctor) makes sense of more immediate activity (e.g., reading a book), particularly when that current action seems at odds with what is immediately advantageous. For example, our reading adolescent continues with his studies in preparation for the morning exam even though his roommates ask him to go out for a drink because the long-term goal outweighs the immediate attraction of grabbing that drink. Similarly, narratives within robust relationships can draw the adolescent to see his current action in light of his longer-term hopes. By asking the simple question, What do you hope for your life? we prompt him to look up from the immediate and construct a story of himself in five or ten years. Like the novice racer, he may be too attracted to distractions immediately in front of him to choose well for the long term or the greater good. He may need us to recognize how one step leads to the next, and leads to the one after that, and either contributes to or detracts from his greater strategy. Through the robust relationship, we provide the questions to prompt the narrative, the patience to bring it to birth, and the perspective toward a larger horizon.

Through the robust relationship, we can also offer compelling narratives of people who have denied themselves for the sake of the greater good, thus creating an imaginative space for the potential consequence of the adolescent's life. An example is that of Dorothy Day. While known for living among and working for the poor, her commitment to promoting human dignity and working for the greater good can be seen in her writing and activism. As a cofounder and contributor to the *Catholic Worker* newspaper, Day advocated for deep structural change in American society. Likewise, her acts of civil disobedience put her own safety at risk but were done to promote the dignity of all lives. The Christian tradition is full of such stories of saints who have done likewise. It will take time, but through compelling stories of others, we might shift the adolescent's perspective from the immediate and self-serving toward a greater good.

MAKING COURSE CORRECTIONS

Even as a long-term strategy of living in love is named, sometimes a given tactic does not work out as expected. For example, our young student, despite his studying, fails his exam, discovering also that he finds biology incomprehensible, thus ending his prospects for medical school. However, if he were invited to revisit his greater hope (to be of aid to people), he might imagine a new and more appropriate way to accomplish that goal that is better suited to his abilities and interests. Returning to a wider narrative horizon helps make sense of, prioritize, and reorganize immediate actions and creates a means by which he can be true to himself while still adaptable.

Sometimes a course correction looks like a complete reversal, as in the case of the apostle Paul. In Acts, Paul recounts his own story of turning from persecution of "this Way" to preaching on behalf of Christ

(Acts 22:4). While seemingly a reversal of direction, Paul tells how he remained "zealous for God" even as his understanding of what that required changed (22:3). His story is clearly one of *metanoia*, but in this address to the Jews of Jerusalem, Paul uses the wider story to show his continued faithfulness to God. Yet, by admitting that "while the blood of your witness Stephen was shed, I myself was standing by, approving and keeping the coats of those who killed him" (22:20), Paul acknowledged that his prior course of action was not free of sin. While not all course corrections are as dramatic as Paul's, for the adolescent who has heard that life should be lived with no regrets or mistakes, it also becomes a story of God's grace that makes any course correction possible.

FINDING MY STORY WITHIN THE LARGER STORY

While forgiveness may sound like a promising idea, we can only forgive ourselves of sin or mistakes if the world in which we live allows for it. MacIntyre writes that "the agent is not only an actor but an author… co-authors of our own narratives. Only in fantasy do we live the story we please….We enter upon a stage which we did not design and we find ourselves part of an action that is not of our making."[25] While the star of our own story, we are supporting actors of someone else's. "Each of our dramas exerts constraints on each other's, making the whole different from the parts, but still dramatic."[26] We are not isolated individuals, but mutually impacting one another. By inviting the adolescent into a narrative of reconciling love and providing him with credible and compelling stories of our own course corrections, we invite him to make sense of and imagine possibilities for his own life. As quoted earlier, MacIntyre writes, "Deprive children of stories and you leave them unscripted, anxious stutters in their actions as in their words."[27] Providing the wider Christian narrative—and not presuming the adolescent knows it already—helps him recognize the foundations upon which we all stand. It invites him to be about something greater than himself, and it prompts him to recognize how he is part of the whole.

Such was the case of Oscar Romero. Upon his installation as archbishop of San Salvador, the country's elite assumed the quiet, scholarly, and conservative priest would become their ally. However, once he understood his role as pastor of *all* the people, he was confronted with the reality of the poverty and injustice in El Salvador. He became a powerful and steadfast advocate for the poor and critic of the elite.

118

Though Romero was assassinated in 1980, his memory has continued to inspire the people. His story is also one of *metanoia*, as he came to a greater appreciation of what was demanded of his role as a bishop faithful to God, he corrected his course.[28]

DEVELOPING INTEGRITY

Finally, MacIntyre uses the concept of narration to argue for some cohesion across a life. MacIntyre recognizes what he calls the "social obstacles…in which modernity partitions each human life into a variety of segments, each with its own norms and modes of behavior. So work is divided from leisure, private life from public, the corporate from the personal."[29] He argues that even though we live in different arenas, our lives are pulled together in something of a uniform narrative, in which we play our own central character. Through the stories we tell, we connect the pieces of our lives, we connect our intentions across settings, and we compose a single narrative that organizes the whole.

For the adolescent who is only beginning to see how expectations differ across his relationships and social settings, it is not unusual for his behavior to appear contradictory across those settings or for him to express different moral frameworks in different settings. In one sense, it demonstrates an accomplishment that he has come to recognize and respond to the expectations of different settings. But we are left—rightly so—distressed at his lack of integrity across those settings because he remains largely unreliable.[30] Within the robust relationship, we can call him to see that the Christian narrative is not reserved for Christian settings but expresses a belief about all life. Like Peter, who knew to look to Jesus for help as he stepped out of the safety of the boat (see Matt 14:30), the adolescent can learn to rely on Jesus even in contrary and frightening settings.

While we do not expect all people to acknowledge the veracity of the Christian narrative themselves, it does shape how we interpret and respond to the world.[31] Religious sister Simone Campbell serves as a contemporary example of someone who lives with integrity across diverse spheres. Her advocacy for the poor, through political lobbying and policy writing, attempts to translate Christian belief about human dignity to policies that support the poor and marginalized. She does not alter her Christian values when she enters the political sphere but finds a way to communicate Christian values with those who believe differently.[32]

Conclusion

The adolescent's sense of her future is shaped by the community's sense of possibility. MacIntyre writes, "We live our lives, both individually and in our relationship with each other, in the light of certain conceptions of a possible shared future….Nonetheless our lives have a certain form which projects itself toward our future."[33] For the adolescent to perceive her life as a gift, she needs others to name it as such. The robust relationship embodies for the adolescent God's very particular love for her, even as God is not limited by it. The relationship invites the adolescent to discover the unique gift of her life by discovering how her life impacts others. She is not lost in the crowd or expected to conform to some abstract image of holiness, but to learn how God comes to fuller life within her. Theologian Elizabeth Johnson writes of the gift of grace as prompting discovery rather than loss of self:

> This gift [of grace], which is not some third thing between God and a person but a gracious offer to participate in the very life of trinitarian communion, heals, redeems, and liberates a person when it is received and responded to from the depths of one's heart…this justifying and sanctifying relation in grace, much more deeply personal, restores a person to one's own true self.[34]

Returning to the example of Paul, who preached to the Corinthians that he "decided to know nothing among you except Jesus Christ, and him crucified" (1 Cor 2:2), yet he remained ever Paul. Likewise, Francis, Dorothy, Oscar, Simone, all remain themselves. Each one is a specific life and unique gift to the world. Within robust relationships, the adolescent can come to see and hear how diverse Christians attempt to live within the world yet remain faithful to God's call to love. Furthermore, the robust relationship offers her a space to compose an integrated narrative of her life, even while she crosses settings. She then has some strategy by which to direct her life. And from within that strategy, she is better able to determine which tactics will contribute to her meeting her goal.

9

Learning to Sail
from Sailors

It takes a great deal of work to learn how to sail well. Sailing is deceptively simple and endlessly complex. It requires catching the wind on a sail so as to move a boat through water. Simple. However, knowing how that wind interacts with the sail, how that sail is trimmed to the boat, how that boat is positioned in the water, and how that water is behaving all factor into sailing well. These factors are in continuous flux, making sailing endlessly complex. Even the expert sailor is never done learning and practicing. Learning to sail well does not happen by chance but requires intentional effort on and off the water. Reading books will help, but it is necessary to get out on the water to try things out and learn the feel of sailing. In fact, it is the back-and-forth movement from practice on the water, to conversation with skilled sailors, to the texts, and back to the water that makes the learning most profitable. Furthermore, practice on the water is best spent in the company of an experienced skipper who is willing to take time to explain and to let the novice try his hand at the various tasks. In fact, the single most valuable element of the learning process is the invitation of that experienced skipper. Through that invitation, the skipper is not only sharing her knowledge, she is also entrusting her boat and perhaps her welfare to the novice. Were it not for generous skippers, there would be fewer sailors in the world. There is a need for such generous skippers in the church.

In addition to helping adolescents reach maturity, Christian communities desire to bring adolescents more deeply into discipleship, the life of the community, and relationship with God.[1] However, part of the challenge of meeting that desire is that the adult members are inviting the adolescent into an "apprenticeship in the entire Christian life" of which they themselves "do not yet have full understanding."[2] Simply put, the adult members of the community frequently do not feel adequate to the task, for they will themselves never master the life of faith and love. They, too, are still learning. Furthermore, the culture of individualism encourages adult members to think that adolescents do not need or want companionship or instruction. The cultural practices of isolation (e.g., frequent travel, full schedules, and constant communication) keep many adults and adolescents from having sufficient unstructured time together within which they notice and know about each other's lives. Because there is so much working against the natural occurrence of robust relationships, Christian communities must think strategically about how they might encourage and support them within their settings. Then those relationships, embedded within the larger community, create what Robert Kegan calls "holding environments," in which individual adolescents are supported and challenged to grow to maturity.[3] In this last chapter, we consider how robust relationships help adolescents grow in the practices of relating, and how ecclesial communities might support the development of robust relationships among mature adults and adolescents.

Practicing the Tactics of Relating

We are never experts in the skills of relating and, as argued previously, we need others to help us in our practice. Relating well takes constant practice such that the practices become habitual. Philosopher Alasdair MacIntyre defines virtue as "an acquired human quality the possession and exercise of which tends to enable us to achieve those goods which are internal to practices and lack of which effectively prevents us from achieving any such goods."[4] For example, I suggest that the practice of patience will only bring forth its benefits (new opportunities, greater understanding, empathy, humility) in the extended practice of patience. If, however, we *think* ourselves patient, but in fact are quick to judge or react, we do not receive these benefits. The practices of relating in love can become such virtuous practices; we grow in our capacity to love by practicing love. We are never experts in relating in love, but the more we practice, the more skilled we become and the greater the benefits.

Theologian Edward Hahnenberg writes, "It is not God who needs a narrative—we do."[5] In the same way, the church community needs practices that train its members to recognize and respond to God's love. The love of God is ever present as grace, but love grows as we participate in it.[6] When shared, love is not divided but multiplied. For humans, however, trusting in the expansive and saving love of God is endlessly challenging. Perhaps it is a factor of our created nature that we are constantly forgetful or unsure of that love. Remembering God's love for us must be practiced so as to work as a force against our natural forgetfulness or insecurity. Likewise, we must practice loving others for them to receive love's benefit. Such practices of remembering and giving are found in liturgy, Scripture, prayer, outreach, advocacy, service, and the life of community. Simply, the giving and receiving of love must be practiced so as to become habitual and to shape our hearts, minds, and strength. For we get good at what we practice, and we never get good at what we do not practice.

The adolescent needs the community and the robust relationships therein to learn and invest in the practices of relating in love, so that she might gain the "goods internal to the practice."[7] By inviting the adolescent into the loving practices of relating, the community extends its own capacity for loving discipleship. In this section, we identify a few practices in the context of robust relationships in a loving community that assist the adolescent in decentering herself such that she can come to see herself better, recognize the personhood of the other, and respond lovingly in her relationship with the other.

LISTENING AND SPEAKING FOR UNDERSTANDING

In chapter 7, we noted the need for the adolescent to become open to the other, starting with those close at hand and expanding to those more distant and different. An essential practice of openness to the other is listening and speaking for understanding. Good listening and speaking is a work in reciprocity, whereby the adolescent misunderstands and understands in turn. Both practices begin with the surprising realization by the adolescent that others do not see the world as he does. They do not live in his head and share his thoughts and experiences.

Philosopher Hans-Georg Gadamer argues that we are always coming to understanding from a place of bias and preunderstanding. Such is the starting place of knowing.[8] So we cannot fault the adolescent for presuming that another person approaches the world as he does, seeing and feeling what he sees and feels. In fact, it is only in the exchange of listening and speaking that he discovers that others hold differing perspectives from his own, and his biases "catch [him] up short."[9] At that moment, Gadamer argues that the adolescent will be challenged to intentionally put his bias aside to hear anew what the other offers. By listening closely to what they really say, he will learn that they have different ideas, histories, social locations, likes and dislikes, and diverse ways of talking. By suspending his presumptions and attending closely to the other, his perspective will be broadened. The basic challenge for the adolescent is to learn to understand others on their terms, and not simply as reflections or extensions of him.

Likewise, in his effort to be understood by the other, the adolescent becomes clearer to himself. Gadamer writes that "the path of all knowledge leads through the question…[and that] the essence of the question is to have a sense…of direction….A question places what is questioned in a particular perspective."[10] Gadamer argues that the question—and the questioner—has its own horizon. By recognizing the question of the other, the adolescent must look at his own story from the perspective of the other. Thus he sees his own story from a new direction and must speak toward that direction, and so recounting something new in the process. He develops his own voice and story as he speaks to another who does not live in his head and heart. As he comes to see himself in relationship to another, he comes to see his particularity and distinctiveness with greater clarity.[11]

Robust relationships become valuable places for the adolescent to learn how to listen and speak. An adolescent may be quick to point out when he is being dismissed or misunderstood but is slow to recognize when he is doing the same. The robust relationship provides a place where he finds another is listening to him, and where he is being challenged to listen to another. The relationship provides opportunities for sustained and meaningful conversation, thus creating opportunities for the ongoing practice of listening and speaking. The adolescent will welcome the chance to test his voice and ideas with the nonparental adult, hoping for greater openness than he might expect from his parents. But the relationship also provides him the space and opportunity to hear the concerns and perspective of an adult. In time, the benefits of listening and speaking for understanding become obvious to the adolescent, and they become virtuous practices that he extends to other relationships.

MAKING ROOM FOR
VULNERABILITY AND FORGIVENESS

Those who succeed at speaking and listening do so because they have kept trying even as they have made mistakes, not because they have spoken perfectly the first time. Listening and speaking are practices that develop with time and effort, so space must be given or created for the practices to develop. When differences between interlocutors become obvious, it is not uncommon to stop speaking, imagining a barrier too high or too uncomfortable to surmount.[12] Both speaking and listening well involve risk and are, therefore, vulnerable acts. Even though the conversational process hopes to arrive at understanding, it usually passes through misunderstanding along the way. Constructive conversation asks us to be comfortable with the discomfort, uncertainty, and frustration that can accompany the effort.

Educator Nicholas Burbules writes of the emotional factors and communicative virtues that support effective communication, especially with those who are different. The emotional factors—like concern, trust, and respect—"are crucial to the bond that sustains a dialogical relationship over time" and through difficulty.[13] Similarly, the virtues—like tolerance, patience, admitting to mistakes—create a space wherein interlocutors have a chance to grow in understanding. These virtues, Burbules argues, are somewhat "context-sensitive"; in those settings wherein these virtues exist, good communication is more likely to happen. In those settings where these virtues are not practiced, it is difficult to speak and listen honestly.[14] For example, Burbules writes, "While one would identify an openness to critical questions from others as generally a communicative virtue, this might be simply too much to ask from persons who have been psychologically demoralized to the point where such criticism is regarded as a threat."[15]

For the adolescent accustomed to digitally mediated communication, these virtues and emotional considerations may seem out of reach. Robust relationships can offer the face-to-face space wherein these virtues are expressed and fostered, thus allowing for appropriate vulnerability. Furthermore, adults can invite difficult conversation by being comfortable with discomfort. And when misunderstandings arise, the adult can give the adolescent the benefit of the doubt, before jumping to more injurious judgments, and encourage the adolescent to do likewise. The adult can practice and encourage forgiveness and reconciliation, and by doing so, expand the space for other relational practices.

RESPONDING WITH DIGNITY AND CARE

Practices of conversation, vulnerability, and forgiveness are not ends in themselves but lead the adolescent to recognize the dignity and personhood of the other and help him learn to respond with care and love to that other. While the adolescent is called to respond in love to each person, the appropriate response may be very particular to the context and relationship (e.g., teacher, boss, friend, and colleague). In each case, responding with care requires an understanding of the other, which itself may call for vulnerability and forgiveness. The adolescent is called to constantly extend that consideration and practice to everyone, even to the extent of serving as neighbor to one he might consider an enemy (cf. Luke 10:25–37).

As discussed in chapter 7, encounters with the other serve as opportunities for God to interrupt the life of the adolescent. While any interruption may be disruptive, Hahnenberg pushes the idea further by arguing that followers of Christ are particularly called to be "interrupted" by the poor. Drawing on liberation theologian and martyr Ignacio Ellacuría, Hahnenberg writes, "Ellacuría argued that the poor represented the privileged place for encountering the reign of God in history."[16] For the poor, like Jesus, are "put to death;…[their] poverty is a reality that is actively inflicted, and thus so is the death that comes with it."[17] Referring to the life and death of Jesus, Hahnenberg writes, "It was a life of loving concern for the poor and the marginalized that challenged the oppressive structures of his day, engendering fierce opposition, and ultimately led to his death. To be a disciple is to carry forward Jesus' mission in our own context."[18] Christians must listen to the poor, suffering, and those who are marginalized to discover how to live in solidarity with them. As Hahnenberg writes, "We need to catch up with them. We, like the Samaritan, must cross over and place ourselves alongside the other in need. There we become a neighbor by loving our neighbor, and so find salvation."[19] The adolescent, like the

Samaritan, needs to be on the lookout for those who are suffering and attend to the suffering as he is able.

The robust relationship helps the adolescent develop the practices of recognizing the dignity of the other and responding in care in at least three ways. First, the adult within the robust relationship calls the adolescent to recognize the adult's personhood and respond in love. Second, through her practice, the adult models and calls the adolescent to practice the skills of communication and attention to the other. Third, the adult invites the adolescent to join the adult in constantly looking out for and responding to the poor, suffering, and marginalized person. Just as the Samaritan and the innkeeper assisted in the care of the victim on the road (see Luke 10:25–37), so too, within the robust relationship the adolescent can learn that care for others is not a solo operation.

Sustaining These Practices

The practices identified here cannot be sustained alone. The adolescent—like us all—needs a community in which to grow and refine the practices. MacIntyre reminds us that

> [the practice's] goods can only be achieved by subordinating ourselves within the practice in our relationship to other practitioners. We have to learn to recognize what is due to whom; we have to be prepared to take whatever self-endangering risks are demanded along the way; and we have to listen carefully to what we are told about our own inadequacies and to reply with the same carefulness for the facts. In other words, we have to accept as necessary components of any practice with internal goods and standards of excellence the virtues of justice, courage, and honesty.[20]

For the adolescent, this means becoming more deeply initiated into the communion of saints, where each contributes another practice of love. For the practices of love are not learned, perfected, or sustained in isolation. Rather, those of any single community member benefits from the practices of other community members, even across centuries. I am sustained by you, and you by me, and those with me.

The importance of the community and ancient practices puts me in mind of sailing large boats. Small boats, operated by one or two people, are limited in where and under what conditions they can safely sail. Underneath the boat there is only a centerboard, which helps with steering, but provides no counterweight. Rather, the body weight of the sailor is used to counter the force of the wind on the sails. Such small boats capsize easily and so are limited in the kind of weather in which they can safely sail. However, larger boats are built with keels. The keel is the heavy protuberance on the bottom of the boat that serves as a counterweight to the force of the wind on the sails. On larger boats, the combined weight of the keel and the several crew members function to keep the boat upright, even in strong winds. Similarly, the Christian community, with its membership and ancient practices, functions like the counterweight of keel and crew, stabilizing the individual when conditions are challenging. Likewise, the individual believer is not depending on himself alone to survive through difficulties but on the company of others and an ancient tradition for ballast.

Toward that end there are parallel practices within the church that initiate, support, and grow the relational practices previously named. By connecting adolescents with these practices, we provide them with valuable resources that endure over time and space. Christian educator Fred Edie argues for the immersion of youth within the liturgical life of the church:

> We have two millennia of accounts, prescriptions, and communal inspiration and wisdom about Christian worship—a veritable treasure trove of liturgical patterns and practices that can redirect our present infatuation with ourselves and our own amusement. This liturgical treasure trove is a means by which youth can be recreated, free from the disproportionate influence of individualism, and through which their attentions and passions can be redirected to resist the unfettered consumptions of goods and experiences designed for personal amusement.[21]

If Christian communities look to the practices within the community, they will recognize those that support the development of loving relationships among its membership, with the world beyond, and with God.

For example, the Christian use of Scripture, especially liturgically, develops the practice of listening. As biblical texts are encountered again and again, they are increasingly heard on the text's terms. Of course, any adolescent who attends liturgy regularly enough will complain, "They read the same thing over and over again." Assuming she already knows what the texts say, the adolescent fails to listen closely. Her presumption of foreknowledge closes her ears from hearing and understanding. However, reading, proclaiming, studying, reflecting, and praying with the Scripture trains the listener to hear it anew each time. The practice of listening and listening again creates new opportunities to understand what has previously been hidden.

Within the Christian practice of song and prayer, we practice speech toward God that leads to deeper understanding of ourselves. Paul writes,

> Likewise the Spirit helps us in our weakness; for we do not know how to pray as we ought, but that very Spirit intercedes with sighs too deep for words. And God, who searches the heart, knows what is the mind of the Spirit, because the Spirit intercedes for the saints according to the will of God. (Rom 8:26–27)

Through psalms, hymns, liturgy, and other prayer forms, the ancient communion of saints, who have been this way before, provide rich language by which we make sense of our way now. Over time, we unpack the word's meanings and recognize our connection to them. Likewise, the adolescent practices listening deeply within herself to discover what needs to be spoken. Through practices of silent contemplation, joyful praise, as well as shared song, she trains her heart to hear what the Spirit is speaking within her.

Similarly, the practice of Eucharist, whereby we are called to recognize the presence of Christ in the elements of bread and wine, trains us to honor the presence of God found outside of gold vessels and tabernacles. Eucharistic practices train believers to recognize and honor the presence of the body of Christ more widely. Finally, sacramental practices of healing and reconciliation train us to acknowledge our frailty and limitations. Rather than endlessly pursuing the route of human effort, we learn to listen for and participate in God's graceful movement.

Robust Relationships

Unfortunately, it has become normal for many communities to respond to the needs of adolescents by creating separately designated times and spaces for them, even for worship, so that they might spend time with their age peers and receive the attention of ministers dedicated to them. While adolescents benefit from dedicated spaces and times — just as elders, parents, men or women's groups do — if these are the exclusive or primary means by which adolescents are served, these efforts will not succeed in integrating them into the life of the larger community. Rather than a bridge to adult faith and membership, it becomes a bridge to nowhere. Christian educator, David White, argues that youth are often "marginalized by the faith communities" when they are sequestered to separate spaces and times and not invited into the larger life of the community.[22] Furthermore, having one person or a small group, no matter how dynamic and accessible, responsible for creating and maintaining close relationships with every adolescent within the community is not only untenable, it is unhealthy, particularly for the minister who may end up feeling overwhelmed and isolated from the larger adult community. Creating and building robust relationships with every adolescent within a community is not the work of paid staff or specialists alone. However, it can be the role of such leaders to create the space and develop the culture in which such relationships are encouraged and made possible among the wider community of adults and adolescents.

The Christian community can create spaces in which each adolescent has the opportunity of being *seen*, *known*, and *valued* by members of the larger community. There is no guarantee that the adolescent will feel that she belongs to a Christian community simply because she is physically present or was present as a child. Nor is it sufficient for her to be seen simply as one of the crowd of young people. If she is to develop a sense of her own personhood, she must be seen for herself, which requires a relationship with someone who sees, knows, and values her. As discussed in chapter 6, the development of new cognitive capacities, particularly the rise of self-consciousness, enable the early adolescent to see herself as a person distinct from the relationships that surround her. She will waver back and forth between thinking she is invisible and thinking everyone is watching her. Thus it becomes important, and differently than as a child, that the adolescent is *seen* as a person in her own right, noticed for herself. She enters a crowded room and someone acknowledges that she is there. She is not part of the furniture, nor a functionary of some role, nor an extension of the other, nor otherwise invisible. In addition to being someone's daughter, classmate, companion, employee, student, niece, or whatever, she becomes someone in her own right and valued as a member of the community.

As argued in chapter 5, the adolescent comes to recognize that value is a socially held commodity. So not only is it important that another person sees the adolescent, the adolescent also needs to acknowledge the other as valuable in order for the adolescent to appreciate the other's recognition. Philosopher Charles Taylor, in *The Ethics of Authenticity*, argues that she does not claim her value for herself; it is always posited in relationship to others.[23] Therefore she is looking for valuable people to notice her, and for adolescents, adults in general hold such value simply by being adults. Even if initially uncomfortable with an adult's recognition—especially unsolicited—she appreciates it. Her apparent embarrassment has more to do with her not knowing what to do with the attention than her not really wanting it.[24]

Once she is seen, the opportunity is opened for the adolescent being *known* and *valued* for who she is. A persistent question, which first rises in adolescence—and can endure for life—is this: "If you really knew me would you still love me?" Being seen is not enough. The adolescent also needs to be *known* and *valued* for who she is, on her own terms; not simply for what she does, or who other people think she is or project onto her. The danger of being known is that it could go either way; there are no assurances of value. Being known holds the risk of rejection and is the greatest reason the adolescent may hide herself or present a self that is more pleasing to those with whom she wishes to connect or maintain relationships like parents, valuable social groups, or romantic interests. But the consequences of withholding can also be significant, as the adolescent may live with the perception that her value in their eyes is provisional. If that presumption is untested, it functions as reality, and she continues to live in that provisional space. Thus it is essential that she have reliable people with whom she can test the waters, with whom disclosure does not feel like such high stakes.[25]

A robust relationship with a mature adult who serves as an honest broker allows the adolescent to test reality. For being seen, known, and valued for oneself does not happen in a crowd, but within smaller settings and enduring relationships with specific people. A robust relationship is prompted when a mature adult notices and authentically expresses interest in the adolescent and calls the adolescent to share something of herself. The adult may invite her to safely and appropriately self-disclose. This adult serves as a sounding board, hearing and responding to the adolescent, assisting her to imagine how others might respond. The robust relationship is important for the adolescent to discover and affirm a sense of her value by having her value affirmed by another.

While there is a need for affirmation, this does not mean that the relationship is uncritical. In fact, it is the balance of challenge and support (not one or the other) that makes the robust relationship a holding environment.[26] Educator Sharon Parks writes of mentoring as assisting the young adult to see himself and see beyond himself. Mentors help the young adult place his life in a wider framework of meaning and stretch his imagination of how his life might contribute to the life of the world. The mentor helps the young person think both critically and expansively about himself.[27] Within the Christian community, a mentoring relationship would be framed within the infinite horizon of God's love and in relationship with Jesus Christ. While the young person is seen, known, and valued for who he is, the mature adult helps him critically and compassionately discern how God is present and revealing in who he is.

Culture for Robust Relationships

To whom do we look for these robust relationships? Besides coming to see, know, and value an adolescent in one's midst, a robust relationship requires a level of *transparency, time,* and *care and respect,* as raised in chapter 7. It is not necessary for organizations to create a one-to-one match of adolescent to adult; nor is it necessary that it be an exclusive, single relationship that supplies all these elements to an individual over the whole span of adolescence; nor is it important that the interested adult be close in age to those needing companionship; nor that the adult be thought of as cool or be at ease with adolescents in general; nor, in some cases, that the adult even be currently alive. What is necessary is that the adolescent experience from the adult a sense of interest in and care for their life, that they serve as a reliable and honest broker, listening and responding to the adolescent and inviting the adolescent into greater maturity.

However, not every adult is going to be good for this work. Just as every person who owns a sailboat is not a good teaching skipper, not every adult will be suited to the task of intentionally forming a robust relationship with a maturing adolescent. I am regularly amazed at people who buy sailboats, particularly large boats, who do not know how to sail. Perhaps they find a way to make use of their investment, but I would discourage novices from going for a sail with them. Things can go bad quickly in a sailboat and someone needs to be responsible for all others on board as well as the boat. The novice skipper needs to gain and grow confident in his skills before he takes on that responsibility. Similarly, adults may present themselves to companion adolescents into adulthood, but they demonstrate a very limited capacity to be responsible within the context of their own relationships. Again, this is not to exclude less-than-perfect people, but to see the invitation, formation, and support of adults and adolescents as an ongoing task of the ecclesial community.

As discussed in chapters 2 and 3, the culture at large discourages connections between adolescents and nonparenting adults. Therefore, the Christian community needs to pay special attention to fostering a culture in which they are welcome and encouraged. First, leadership can encourage greater openness among and between adults, pointing to the value of nonparent relationships for adolescents. Adults need to be encouraged to be open to the adolescents in their midst, both teenagers and twentysomethings. This may include encouraging parents to allow or invite other adults to form relationships with their sons and daughters.

Second, leadership can recognize the spaces and opportunities wherein robust relationships might grow. Here it is important to look at the whole life and activity of the community. In each setting, ask where and how the membership is interacting and whether the setting allows for or encourages people to see, know, and value one another, and whether there is opportunity for relationships to grow. These opportunities may already be available around the community's liturgical life, educational initiatives, retreats, and outreach and advocacy efforts. It may not require new programming, but new ways of configuring the life of the community.

Third, the leadership can create supports for adults, particularly those that help them notice and respond to the mental, emotional, and physical health of adolescents. Fortunately, most dioceses and schools require some training prior to working with children and adolescents, but this is often focused on those with formal, both paid and unpaid, roles. It is important that the general population of adults feel they are part of a network, able to reach out to appropriate others in the community to support adolescents.

Christian communities might call on their more skilled practitioners to share their knowledge with other mature and maturing adults. A few years ago, I had the opportunity to go to Newport, Rhode Island, to see the six boats competing in the 2015 Volvo Ocean Race. It was a round-the-world race, lasting some months, with only eleven ports, including Newport, en route. I was amazed that these sloop-design boats were similar in their basic functioning to the sailboats I sailed.[28] Likewise, the eight sailors on board were practicing many of the same basic skills that I practice. However, I was incredibly aware that the level of skill they possessed was far superior to mine, allowing them to cross oceans and round the horns of Africa and South America through some of the most dangerous waters on earth. They were highly skilled sailors, tacking and jibing as directed, fulfilling their roles in the team, and taking their turn at the helm. While very able, at some point, they had learned from other sailors. The skills of sailing were passed along from others. Similarly, each ecclesial community has many rich assets within its own membership to grow its capacity for robust relationships with its adolescent members.

Apprenticeship in the Communion of Saints

The church's mission is to live into discipleship. That is not the work only for its youthful members, but for all of us. Therefore, when we apprentice youth into the life of the community, we are apprenticing them into a way of life—into practices that shape how they are in the world and how they see that world.

The image of the communion of saints is helpful and appropriate as we think about the church as present and inviting to adolescents. Theologian Elizabeth Johnson, in *Friends of God and Prophets*, writes, "The *communion sanctorum* is a most relational symbol. From age to age, the same Spirit who vivifies and renews the natural world enters into holy souls, and not so holy ones, and makes them friends of God and prophets."[29] She goes on to identify "five rudimentary elements" of that communion, three of which I raise up for our discussion. They are the following:

> [1] the community of living, ordinary people as "all saints," in particular…members of the Christian community and their relationship to the triune God;…[2] the circle of companions who have run the race before, who are now embraced in the life of God and accessed through memory and hope; and [3] the paradigmatic figures among them.[30]

In her retrieval of the ancient image, Johnson builds on the concept of God's grace as prior to all and present to all, to expand and enrich the image. While this communion of saints lives in unity around faithfulness to God's call, Johnson points to their vast diversity. Diversity in who they were, how they responded in their time and place, and how they were received in their time.

The image of the communion of saints represents the great diversity of the Christian community and is a gift and a benefit to the great diversity of adolescents, younger and older, who we are continually invited into fuller membership within this communion. The presently living Christian community, as a communion of saints, provides the practices of companionship, interpretation, affirmation, and guidance in discerning God's word and movement in the life of the adolescent. Those who have gone before provide models of discernment and discipleship. If they were personally known to the adolescent, the adolescent may hold a memory of care and a hope for ongoing patronage. Those paradigmatic saints ground the adolescent in a historic and inspiring tradition. The communion of saints is a rich image for the whole community—adult and adolescent—

which is brought more deeply into proclaiming, attending, interpreting, and celebrating the story of God's love in their lives.

As we think about the church's ministry to its adolescent membership, it is one of inviting them into mature, loving relationships with themselves, with God, with the church, and with the wider world. The community accomplishes this by recognizing the unique and valuable personhood of the adolescent and by calling the adolescent to recognize, similarly, the personhood of others and respond in love. Both tasks are best accomplished in robust relationships where she will learn to interpret her life and the world upon the horizon of God's infinite love.

Notes

1. The Project of Adolescence

1. Laurence Steinberg, *The Age of Opportunity: Lessons from the New Science of Adolescence* (Boston: Mariner Books, 2014), 19–20. Steinberg offers several theories as to why our memories from adolescence are so vivid.

2. Jeffrey Arnett, *Emerging Adulthood: The Winding Road from the Late Teens to the Twenties* (New York: Oxford University Press, 2004). Sociologist Arnett is chief among those identifying a protracted process, coining the term "emerging adult" for those between eighteen and twenty-eight years old. Robert Epstein, *The Case against Adolescence: Rediscovering the Adult in Every Teen* (Sanger, CA: Quill Driver Books, 2007). Epstein credits the "infantilization of teens" within U.S. culture. John Taylor Gatto, *Dumbing Us Down: The Hidden Curriculum of Compulsory Schooling* (Philadelphia, PA: New Society Publishers, 1992). Gatto blames mandatory schooling practices of the twentieth century.

3. William Damon, *The Path to Purpose: How Young People Find Their Calling in Life* (New York: Free Press, 2008). Damon credits it to a lack of purpose. David Elkind, *All Grown Up and No Place to Go: Teenagers in Crisis*, rev. ed. (Cambridge, MA: De Capo Press, 1998). Elkind implicates changing family structures. Chap Clark, *Hurt: Inside the World of Today's Teenagers* (Grand Rapids, MI: Baker Academic, 2004). Clark credits adult systematic abandonment of youth in favor of adult pursuits.

4. Christian Smith and Melinda Lundquist Denton, *Soul Searching: The Religious and Spiritual Lives of American Teenagers* (New York: Oxford University Press, 2004); Christian Smith, Kyle Longest, Jonathan Hill, and Kari Christoffersen, *Young Catholic America: Emerging Adults In, Out of, and Gone from the Church* (New York: Oxford University Press, 2014); and Thomas Rausch, *Being Catholic in a Culture of Choice* (Collegeville, MN: Liturgical Press, 2006).

5. Peter Langman, *School Shooters: Understanding High School, College, and Adult Perpetrators* (New York: Rowman & Littlefield, 2015). Langman identifies adolescent and college-age school shooters as previously traumatized, psychotic, or psychopathic.

6. Drawing on Wilfred Cantwell Smith, Parks develops the idea of adulthood as "becoming at home in the universe." Sharon Daloz Parks, *Big Questions, Worthy Dreams: Mentoring Young Adults in Their Search for Meaning, Purpose, and Faith* (San Francisco: Jossey-Bass, 2000), 34.

7. Throughout, I alternate among male, female, and gender-neutral pronouns both for the ease of reading and to prompt the reader to imagine the young people of the reader's acquaintance. While valuable, it is beyond the scope of this book to allow for more than passing analysis of how gender, race, ethnicity, or socioeconomic status affect adolescence.

8. John D. Zizioulas, "The Doctrine of the Holy Trinity: The Significance of the Cappadocian Contribution," in *Trinitarian Theology Today: Essays on Divine Being and Act*, ed. Christoph Schwöbel (Edinburgh: T&T Clark, 1995), 55.

9. Zizioulas, "The Doctrine of the Holy Trinity," 55. Emphasis in the original.

10. Zizioulas, "The Doctrine of the Holy Trinity," 50.

11. Zizioulas, "The Doctrine of the Holy Trinity," 56–57. Emphasis in the original.

12. The pursuit of disaffected or isolated adolescents has become a severe problem on several fronts. Christopher Lennings, Krestina Amon, Heidi Brummert, Nicholas Lennings, "Grooming for Terror: The Internet and Young People," *Psychiatry, Psychology and Law* 17 (2010): 424–37; H.J. Clawson, M. Dutch, A. Solomon, and Grace Goldblatt, *Human Trafficking into and within the United States: A Review of the Literature*, (Washington, DC: Office of the Assistant Secretary for Planning and Evaluation, 2009).

13. Catherine Mowry LaCugna, *God for Us: The Trinity and Christian Life* (San Francisco: HarperSanFrancisco, 1991), 302. In this instance, LaCugna is speaking of the "incomprehensibility of God," arguing that God does not hide, but that God as person can never be wholly known.

14. Erik Erikson, *Identity: Youth and Crisis* (New York: W. W. Norton & Co., 1968), 257.

15. Alasdair MacIntyre, *After Virtue: A Study in Moral Theory*, 2nd ed. (Notre Dame, IN: University of Notre Dame Press, 1984), 221. The shaping and informing of personal narrative from the social worlds in which one finds oneself is a central argument of MacIntyre.

16. Charles Taylor, *Sources of the Self: The Making of the Modern Identity* (Cambridge, MA: Harvard University Press, 1989). This is a major argument of the first chapter. A similar argument is made by MacIntyre, *After Virtue*.

17. Hans-Georg Gadamer, *Truth and Method*, 2nd rev. ed. (New York: Continuum, 1999), 302. Gadamer credits Friedrich Nietzsche and Edmund Husserl with first using *horizon* to refer to the "infinite determinacy."

18. Arnett, *Emerging Adulthood*, 133. Such can be read in Arnett's preference for the "American system" of higher education whereby the individual student is able to enter and remain undecided about a course of study. The "American system offers young people more of an opportunity to find the educational and occupational path that will be the right fit for them."

19. Clark, *Hurt*. The opposite extreme is parents making all choices for their adolescent sons and daughters. By doing so, parents communicate a set direction and values, including a belief that the son or daughter is incapable of making such decisions.

20. MacIntyre, *After Virtue*, 209. MacIntyre argues for "the central importance of intelligibility" in human action and discourse. "Human beings can be held to account for that of which they are authors."

21. Sherry Turkle, *Alone Together: Why We Expect More from Technology and Less from Each Other* (New York: Basic Books, 2011), 155.

22. Several voices claim that it is in this breach that market-based interests spring up and flourish, providing for the adolescent a sense of identity and value. Tom Beaudoin, *Consuming Faith: Integrating Who We Are with What We Buy* (Lanham, MD: Sheed & Ward, 2003); and

David White, *Practicing Discernment with Youth: A Transformative Youth Ministry Approach* (Cleveland, OH: The Pilgrim Press, 2005).

23. Christian Smith, Kari Christoffersen, Hilary Davidson, and Patricia Snell Herzog, *Lost in Transition: The Dark Side of Emerging Adulthood* (New York: Oxford University Press, 2011).

24. Karl Rahner, *Foundations of Christian Faith: An Introduction to the Idea of Christianity* (New York: Crossroads, 1978), 20.

25. Rahner, *Foundations of Christian Faith*, 23.

26. Rahner, *Foundations of Christian Faith*, 22.

27. Edward Hahnenberg, *Awakening Vocation: A Theology of Christian Call* (Collegeville, MN: Liturgical Press, 2010), 131.

28. Rahner, *Foundations of Christian Faith*, 86.

29. Rahner, *Foundations of Christian Faith*, 39.

30. Hahnenberg, *Awakening Vocation*, 152.

31. Hahnenberg, *Awakening Vocation*, 173. Throughout this discussion, Hahnenberg draws from Lieven Boeve's concept of "interruption" found in Lieven Boeve, *Interrupting Tradition: An Essay on Christian Faith in a Postmodern Context*, (Louvain: Peeters Press, 2003).

32. Hahnenberg, *Awakening Vocation*, 173.

33. Theresa O'Keefe, "Companioning Adolescents into Adulthood: Schools as Communities of Care and Growth," in *Education Matters: Readings in Pastoral Care for School Chaplains, Guidance Counsellors, and Teachers*, ed. James O'Higgins Norman (Dublin: Veritas Publications, 2014).

34. Elizabeth A. Johnson, *Friends of God and Prophets: A Feminist Theological Reading of the Communion of Saints* (New York: Continuum, 1999), 220.

35. Johnson, *Friends of God and Prophets*, 222.

36. Johnson, *Friends of God and Prophets*, 234.

37. Johnson, *Friends of God and Prophets*, 234.

38. Hahnenberg, *Awakening Vocation*, 131.

2. Sailing Solo

1. For example, the sexualization of youth culture happens within a sexualization within the larger culture. R. Danielle Egan,

Becoming Sexual: A Critical Appraisal of the Sexualization of Girls (Malden, MA: Polity Press, 2013).

2. Robert Putnam, *Bowling Alone: The Collapse and Revival of American Community* (New York: Simon and Schuster, 2000), 24.

3. Robert Bellah, Richard Madsen, William Sullivan, Ann Swidler, and Steven Tipton, *Habits of the Heart: Individualism and Commitment in American Life* (Berkeley, CA: University of California Press, 2008), 56–57.

4. Bellah et al., *Habits of the Heart*, 55.

5. Juliet Schor, *Born to Buy: The Commercialized Child and the New Consumer Culture* (New York: Scribner, 2004). According to Schor, marketers claimed addressing children directly was a more effective means of marketing than trying to reach through parents. See also Schor, *The Overspent American: Why We Want What We Don't Need* (New York: Basic Books, 1998); Vincent Miller, *Consuming Religion: Christian Faith and Practice in a Consumer Culture* (New York: Continuum, 2003); and Tom Beaudoin, *Consuming Faith: Integrating Who We Are with What We Buy* (New York: Sheed & Ward, 2003).

6. Miller, *Consuming Religion*, 109. Vincent Miller argues that contemporary marketing efforts have a tremendous capacity for misdirecting our deep human desires in the pursuit of short-term consumables.

7. Beaudoin, *Consuming Faith*.

8. Laurence Steinberg, *Age of Opportunity: Lessons from the New Science of Adolescence* (Boston: Mariner Books, 2014).

9. Population figures are taken from the United States Census Bureau, accessed June 13, 2017, http://www.census.gov/topics/population.html.

10. Food and Agriculture Organization of the United Nations, "The State of Food Insecurity in the World: Executive Summary 2013," accessed June 13, 2017, http://www.fao.org/docrep/018/i3458e/i3458e.pdf.

11. United States Census Bureau, "World Population: 1950–2050," accessed December 5, 2013, https://www.census.gov/.

12. Norman Pounds, *The Medieval City* (Westport, CT: Greenwood Press, 2005); Fritz Rörig, *The Medieval Town* (Berkeley: University of California Press, 1969); and Office of National Statistics, "London's Population Was Increasing the Fastest among the Regions

in 2012," October 17, 2013, https://www.london.gov.uk/sites/default/files/housing_in_london_2015.pdf.

13. United States Census Bureau, "US and World Population Clock," accessed June 13, 2017, http://www.census.gov/popclock/. The Census Bureau has changed the way urban settings are factored, as the nature of urban settings has changed over the past century.

14. At the beginning of the twentieth century, most people lived in rural settings (1900, at 60.4 percent rural). By the end of the twentieth century, the population has shifted to urban settings (1990, at 75.2 percent urban). United States Census Bureau, "Urban and Rural Populations: 1900–1990," October 1995, http://www.census.gov/population/censusdata/urpop0090.txt.

15. Lee Rainie and Barry Wellman, *Networked: The New Social Operating System* (Cambridge, MA: MIT Press, 2012). These authors draw on research conducted through the Pew Research Center's Internet and American Life Project and NetLab at the University of Toronto.

16. Rainie and Wellman, *Networked*, 125. A major value of social networks is the extension of reach for solving problems, but that places more responsibility for initiating and responding on the individual.

17. Putnam, *Bowling Alone*, 19.

18. Rainie and Wellman, *Networked*, 270. Social capital must be built up to be available to draw down within social networks.

19. Putnam, *Bowling Alone*, 283.

20. Putnam, *Bowling Alone*. Putnam noted a decline in changes of residence of Americans over the later decades of the twentieth century. However, he did note that the sprawl of American lives over vast metropolitan areas (live in one community, work in another, go to school in a third, and shop in a fourth) has increased.

21. Sherry Turkle, *Alone Together: Why We Expect More from Technology and Less from Each Other* (New York: Basic Books, 2011), 155.

22. Parents and grandparents have various motivations for engaging their children in so many activities, from concern for youth safety, developing interests and talents, finding like-minded communities, and growing resumes for college entrance. Many of these may be unwittingly market inspired, pushing parents to do "what's best" without giving them forums for considering what really is best for their child. A great analysis of this market focus on children, youth, and families can be found in Schor, *Born to Buy*.

23. Diana Eck, *A New Religious America: How a "Christian Country" Has Become the World's Most Religiously Diverse Nation* (San Francisco: HarperSanFrancisco, 2002). Eck offers a valuable analysis of this history and its implications for the United States.

24. Theresa O'Keefe, "Growing Up Alone: The New Normal of Isolation in Adolescents," *The Journal of Youth Ministry* 13 (2014): 70–71.

25. For resources on growing up in the late medieval period, see Barbara A. Hanawalt, *Growing Up in Medieval London: The Experience of Childhood in History* (New York: Oxford University Press, 1993); David Herlihy, *Women, Family and Society in Medieval Europe: Historical Essays, 1978-1991* (Providence, RI: Berghahn Books, 1995); Crystal Kirgiss, *In Search of Adolescence: A New Look at an Old Idea* (San Diego, CA: The Youth Cartel, 2015); John Mundy and Peter Reisenberg, *The Medieval Town* (Princeton, NJ: Van Nostrand Co., Inc., 1958); Paul Newman, *Growing Up in the Middle Ages* (Jefferson, NC: McFarland, 2007); Nicholas Orme, *Medieval Children* (New Haven, CT: Yale University Press, 2001); Nicholas Orme, *Medieval Schools: From Roman Britain to Renaissance England* (New Haven, CT: Yale University Press, 2006); and Norman Pounds, *The Medieval City* (Westport, CT: Greenwood Press, 2005).

26. Apprentices to law were a notable exception. They generally lived together in rented rooms, accompanied by their own servants. They were notorious for their rowdiness and drinking. Hanawalt, *Growing Up in Medieval London*, 125.

27. Rainie and Wellman, *Networked*, 34–39.

28. Rainie and Wellman, *Networked*, 135.

29. Rainie and Wellman, *Networked*, 132.

30. Rainie and Wellman, *Networked*, 135.

3. Relying on Instruments

1. Amanda Lenhart, "Teens, Social Media, and Technology Overview 2015," *Pew Research Center: Internet, Science, and Tech*, April 9, 2015, http://www.pewinternet.org/2015/04/09/teens-social-media-technology-2015/.

2. Lenhart, "Teens, Social Media, and Technology Overview 2015."

3. Among the authors who see dire consequences for our digital lives is Giles Slade, *The Big Disconnect: The Story of Technology and Loneliness* (Amherst, NY: Prometheus Books, 2012); and Nicholas Carr, *The Shallows: What the Internet is Doing to Our Brains* (New York: W.W. Norton & Co., 2010).

4. danah boyd, *It's Complicated: The Social Lives of Networked Teens* (New Haven, CT: Yale University Press, 2014), 8.

5. Lee Rainie and Barry Wellman, *Networked: The New Social Operating System* (Cambridge, MA: MIT Press, 2012), 6.

6. Sherry Turkle, *Second Self: Computers and the Human Spirit* (Cambridge, MA: MIT Press, 1984) and *Life on Screen: Identity in the Age of the Internet* (New York: Simon & Schuster, 1985). In her earlier writing, Turkle noted that digital communications (web pages, social media, virtual reality) provided opportunities for people—notably adolescents—to express their identity to wider and different worlds than if they met face-to-face. Turkle, *Alone Together: Why We Expect More from Technology and Less from Each Other* (New York: Basic Books, 2011) and *Reclaiming Conversation: The Power of Talk in a Digital Age* (New York: Penguin Press, 2015). These later works reflect a change of position.

7. Turkle, *Alone Together*, 190.

8. boyd, *It's Complicated*, 18.

9. boyd, *It's Complicated*, 90. boyd finds that the need for free time with friends is a major driver for teen use of technology. Their time is so structured between schooling and outside activities that unlike prior generations of teens, there is little space to "meet and hang out."

10. Shari P. Walsh, Katherine M. White, and Ross M. Young, "The Phone Connection: A Qualitative Exploration of How Belongingness and Social Identification Relate to Mobile Phone Use amongst Australian Youth," *Journal of Community and Applied Social Psychology* 19 (2009): 225–40. See also Turkle, *Alone Together*, 248.

11. Turkle, *Alone Together*, 155–56.

12. Turkle, *Reclaiming Conversation*, 368n4. Turkle points to research that the mere presence of a phone on a table undermines the depth of conversation.

13. boyd, *It's Complicated*, 38.

14. Rainie and Wellman, *Networked*, 141.

15. Rainie and Wellman, *Networked*, 127. They found among adult users "the more internet contacts, the more in-person and phone contact," but they have no evidence of that being the case for adolescents.

16. Turkle, *Alone Together*, 200.

17. Turkle, *Alone Together*, 206.

18. Turkle, *Alone Together*, 190.

19. danah boyd, "Why Youth (Heart) Social Network Sites," in *Youth, Identity and Digital Media*, ed. David Buckingham (Cambridge, MA: MIT Press, 2008), 129.

20. boyd, *It's Complicated*, 8. boyd calls these audiences "networked publics"; they are "the space constructed through networked technologies and the imagined community that emerges as a result of the intersection of people, technology, and practice."

21. boyd, "Why Youth (Heart) Social Network Sites," 126. Additionally, boyd warns that "persistence" and "searchability" are two elements that differentiate network-mediated communication from unmediated. She and Turkle agree that mistakes made stay and are even searchable long after the fact, regardless of the original poster's initial intention and audience. See also Turkle, *Alone Together*, 169.

22. Nicholas Burbles, *Dialogue in Teaching: Theory and Practice* (New York: Teachers College Press, 1993), 43.

23. Theresa O'Keefe, "Learning to Talk: Conversation across Religious Difference," *Religious Education* 104 (2009): 197–213. In other research, I have uncovered the need for trust to develop for potentially difficult topics to be discussed.

24. Susannah Stern, "Producing Sites, Exploring Identities: Youth Online Authorship," in *Youth, Identity, and Digital Media*, ed. David Buckingham (Cambridge, MA: MIT Press, 2008), 101–3.

25. Stern, "Producing Sites, Exploring Identities," 104. Stern finds that technology blurs the line between public and private audiences when teens pursue self-expression and validation. She writes, "Some youth authors think of their communication as private when the people they know in real life do not see, hear, or read it, regardless of who else does."

26. Stern, "Producing Sites, Exploring Identities,"112.

27. Turkle, *Alone Together*, 224.

28. Shaheen Chariff, *Confronting Cyber Bullying: What Schools Need to Know to Control Misconduct and Avoid Legal Consequences* (New York: Cambridge University Press, 2009); Robin Kowalski, *Cyber Bullying: Bullying in the Digital Age* (Malden, MA: Blackwell Publishing, 2008); and Sameer Hinduja and Justin Patchin, *Bullying beyond the Schoolyard: Preventing and Responding to Cyberbullying* (Thousand Oaks, CA: Corwin, 2014).

29. Rainie and Wellman, *Networked*, 270.

30. James Russell, Jo-Ann Bachorowski, and José-Miguel Fernandez-Dols, "Facial and Vocal Expressions of Emotion," *Annual Review of Psychology* 54 (2003): 329–49; and James Russell, "Is There Universal Recognition of Emotion from Facial Expressions? A Review of the Cross-Cultural Studies," *Psychological Bulletin* 115 (1994): 102–41.

31. Stern, "Producing Sites, Exploring Identities," 111–12; boyd, "Why Youth (Heart) Social Network Sites," 129.

32. Turkle, *Alone Together*, 248–51. Turkle recounts the story of a young woman who had invested five years in an online relationship because it was more affirming than her face-to-face relationships. However, she was left wondering if the person on the other end was real.

33. boyd, *It's Complicated*, 129.

34. Turkle, *Alone Together*, 180–82.

35. Rainie and Wellman, *Networked*, 125.

36. Turkle *Alone Together*, 192–98. Turkle offers numerous examples of users who feel their lives online are more real than their lives off-line. See also Rainie and Wellman, *Networked*, 126. They challenge Turkle's finding that people present "second selves" online that are different from their off-line personas. However, they refer to a "networked self: a single self that gets reconfigured in different situations as people reach out, connect, and emphasize different aspects of themselves."

37. Turkle, *Alone Together*, 161.

38. Such is the story of a college student who had an opportunity to walk the Camino de Santiago in northern Spain. He offered this reflection on the practice of silence and the absence of technology over the course of the many days: "This is the longest time I've been with my own thoughts in my life. At home I'm lucky if five minutes pass before I check my phone. Here I can actually feel my train of thought progressing." Zachary Jason, "The Voyage: Jeffrey Bloechl's

Philosophy Class Was a Test of Mind, Heart, and Body," *Boston College Magazine*, Summer 2015, 26.

39. Rainie and Wellman, *Networked*, 143.

40. Rainie and Wellman, *Networked*, 146.

41. Marc Prensky, "Digital Natives, Digital Immigrants, Part I," *On the Horizon* 9 (2001): 1–6, doi.org/10.1108/10748120110424816.

42. Immanuel Levinas, *Totality and Infinity* (Pittsburgh, PA: Duquesne University Press, 1969), 87. Levinas argues that the face of the Other confronts us and makes demands such that we encounter the infinite in them. They cannot be reduced to our ideas of them.

43. Edward Hahnenberg, *Awakening Vocation: A Theology of Christian Call* (Collegeville, MN: Liturgical Press, 2010), 134. Emphasis in the original. Hahnenberg, as an interpreter of Rahner, makes the great theologian's dense work much more accessible and so I use him here.

44. Hahnenberg, *Awakening Vocation*, 134.

45. Karl Rahner, *Foundations of Christian Faith: An Introduction to the Idea of Christianity*, trans. William V. Dych (New York: Crossroad, 1978), 118.

46. Rahner, *Foundations of Christian Faith*, 52–54.

47. Rahner, *Foundations of Christian Faith*, 22.

48. Rahner, *Foundations of Christian Faith*, 22.

49. Rahner, *Foundations of Christian Faith*, 38.

50. Rahner, *Foundations of Christian Faith*, 39.

51. Catherine Mowry LaCugna, *God for Us: The Trinity and Christian Life* (San Francisco, CA: HarperSanFrancisco, 1973), 260.

4. Charting a Course

1. James Holstein and Jaber Gubrim, *The Self We Live By: Narrative Identity in a Postmodern World* (New York: Oxford University Press, 1999), 10–11. My thinking here has been informed by Holstein and Gubrim, who propose that the self "is a social construction that we both assemble and live out as we take up or resist the demands of everyday life. This is an eminently practical and socially variegated self."

2. Robert Epstein, *The Case against Adolescence: Rediscovering the Adult in Every Teen* (Sanger, CA: Quill Driver Books, 2007); and

Jeffrey Arnett, *Emerging Adulthood: The Winding Road from the Late Teens to the Twenties* (New York: Oxford University Press, 2004).

3. The average age of marriage for men in 1890 was 26.1 years old. Joseph Kett, *Rites of Passage: Adolescence in America 1790 to the Present* (New York: Basic Books, 1977), 247. In 1950, it was twenty-two, and in 2000, it was twenty-seven. See also Arnett, *Emerging Adulthood*, 4–5.

4. Arnett, *Emerging Adulthood*, 14. Arnett asks his interview subjects if they feel like an adult without suggesting any parameters by which they might imagine or define adulthood. This is problematic in that it suggests that adulthood, childhood, or any life stage for that matter, is determined by the individual without reference to anything outside his or her own imagination. That valid interpretation is done in isolation without reference to external voices. While such a question may elicit the interview subject's impression, it cannot offer a valid definition of adulthood.

5. Arnett, *Emerging Adulthood*, 210. In his studies with young adults between eighteen and twenty-nine, Arnett consistently found that responsibility, care for others, and thinking for oneself were reported as essential for adulthood. Robert Kegan, *In Over Our Heads: The Mental Demands of Modern Life* (Cambridge, MA: Harvard University Press, 1994) and *The Evolving Self: Problem and Process in Human Development* (Cambridge, MA: Harvard University Press, 1982). Kegan identifies these as the expectations put on adolescents as they move toward adulthood.

6. Arnett, *Emerging Adulthood*, 6.

7. Arnett, *Emerging Adulthood*, 14. A study subject quoted by Arnett claimed, "I'll know I'm an adult when I don't eat ice cream right out of the box anymore!" Yet she goes on to describe her consistently responsible behavior at work and financially. Arnett never challenges this conception of adulthood the young woman holds, when in fact many responsible adults eat ice cream out of the box without consequence to their status as adults.

8. Holstein and Gubrium, *The Self We Live By*, 70. Holstein and Gubrium, interpreting Jean-François Lyotard, write, "The truths of objects like the self are matters of local discursive recognition." The "language game" of the setting creates the frame of reference within which members make choices about how they will describe and so create what is real and valuable for that setting.

9. Linda Borgen and Ruben G. Rumbaut, "Coming of Age in 'America's Finest City': Transitions to Adulthood among Children of

Immigrants in San Diego," in *Coming of Age in America: The Transition to Adulthood in the Twenty-First Century*, eds. Mary C. Waters et al. (Berkley, CA: University of California Press, 2011), 166–67.

10. Within the Commonwealth of Massachusetts, I am familiar with the efforts of the Department of Developmental Services to assist in such negotiation on behalf of citizens with limited cognitive and physical abilities. They work to enhance the self-determination and responsibility of adults with limited abilities while working with others in their context to meet responsibilities that the individual is unable to meet alone.

11. Catherine Mowry LaCugna, *God for Us: The Trinity and Christian Life* (San Francisco: HarperSanFrancisco, 1991), 213.

12. LaCugna, *God for Us*, 254. Seventeenth-century philosopher René Descartes is attributed with accenting a divide between the rational mind and the body.

13. LaCugna, *God for Us*, 255.

14. LaCugna, *God for Us*, 292.

15. LaCugna, *God for Us*, 256.

16. LaCugna, *God for Us*, 257.

17. LaCugna, *God for Us*, 260.

18. LaCugna, *God for Us*, 261.

19. LaCugna, *God for Us*, 261.

20. LaCugna, *God for Us*, 263.

21. LaCugna, *God for Us*, 265.

22. LaCugna, *God for Us*, 266. LaCugna points to relationships of inequality based on gender, race, and socioeconomic status.

23. LaCugna, *God for Us*, 271. Emphasis in the original.

24. LaCugna, *God for Us*, 271.

25. LaCugna, *God for Us*, 271.

26. LaCugna, *God for Us*, 277.

27. LaCugna, *God for Us*, 284.

28. LaCugna, *God for Us*, 280.

5. Discovering a Horizon

1. Sharon Daloz Parks, *Big Questions, Worthy Dreams: Mentoring Young Adults in Their Search for Meaning, Purpose, and Faith* (San

Francisco: Jossey-Bass, 2000), 34. Similarly, Parks writes of adulthood as "becoming at home in the universe." She draws this from Wilfred Cantwell Smith, *Faith and Reason* (Princeton, NJ: Princeton University Press, 1979), 12.

2. Juliet Schor, *Born to Buy: The Commercialized Child and the New Consumer Culture* (New York: Scribner, 2004). Schor's research unmasks the efforts to which marketers go to manufacture "cool" and make it look like the consumer's idea. Helga Dittmar, Rod Bond, Megan Hurst, and Tim Kasser, "The Relationship between Materialism and Personal Well-Being: A Meta-Analysis," *Journal of Personality and Social Psychology* 107 (2014): 879–924.

3. Sherry Turkle, *Reclaiming Conversation: The Power of Talk in a Digital Age* (New York: Penguin Press, 2015), 200. Technology researcher Sherry Turkle reports on the "interpretive weight" carried by punctuation within texting.

4. Tom Beaudoin, *Consuming Faith: Integrating Who We Are with What We Buy* (Lanham, MD: Sheed & Ward, 2003). Beaudoin writes of the deep attention to sign value that is at the heart of consumer branding, thus making marketing more than the selling of products, but of identity.

5. Charles Taylor, *Sources of the Self: The Making of the Modern Identity* (Cambridge, MA: Harvard University Press, 1989), 36.

6. Erik Erikson, *Identity: Youth and Crisis* (New York: W.W. Norton, 1968), 233.

7. Erikson, *Identity*, 241. Erikson speaks of the need to feel one's life has a sense of consequence.

8. Donna Freitas, *Sex and the Soul: Juggling Sexuality, Spirituality, Romance and Religion on America's College Campus* (New York: Oxford University Press, 2008); Michael Kimmel, *Guyland: The Perilous World Where Boys Become Men* (New York: HarperCollins, 2008); and Jason King, *Faith with Benefits: Hookup Culture on Catholic Campuses* (New York: Oxford University Press, 2017).

9. Alasdair MacIntyre, *After Virtue: A Study in Moral Theory*, 2nd ed. (Notre Dame, IN: University of Notre Dame Press, 1984), 219.

10. Christian Smith, Kari Christoffersen, Hilary Davidson, and Patricia Snell Herzog, *Lost in Transition: The Dark Side of Emerging Adulthood* (New York: Oxford University Press, 2011); and William Damon, *The Path to Purpose: How Young People Find Their Calling in Life* (New York: Free Press, 2008).

Notes

11. Robert N. Bellah, Richard Madsen, William M. Sullivan, Ann Swidler, and Steven M. Tipton, *Habits of the Heart: Individualism and Commitment in American Life* (Berkeley, CA: University of California Press, 2008); and Robert Putnam, *Bowling Alone: The Collapse and Revival of American Community* (New York: Simon & Schuster, 2000).

12. Vincent Miller, *Consuming Religion: Christian Faith and Practice in a Consumer Culture* (New York: Continuum, 2005).

13. Robert Kegan, *In over Our Heads: The Mental Demands of Modern Life* (Cambridge, MA: Harvard University Press, 1994). This is explained in detail in chapter 6.

14. William Damon, *The Path to Purpose: How Young People Find Their Calling in Life* (New York: Free Press, 2008), 105.

15. Damon, *The Path to Purpose*, 33.

16. Damon, *The Path to Purpose*, 108.

17. Peter C. Scales, Peter L. Benson, and Mark Mannes, "The Contribution to Adolescent Well-Being Made by Nonfamily Adults: An Examination of Developmental Assets as Contexts and Processes," *Journal of Community Psychology* 34 (2006): 401–13; and Eva Oberle, Kimberly Schonert-Reichl, and Bruno Zumbo, "Life Satisfaction in Early Adolescence: Personal, Neighborhood, School, Family, and Peer Influences," *Journal of Youth and Adolescence* 40 (2011): 889–901. There is a large and growing body of research on the link between relationships and positive youth development, best accessed through the Search Institute, a research and resource organization dedicated to positive youth development. See http://www.search-institute.org/.

18. Belle Laing, Allison White, Angela DeSilva Mousseau, Alexandra Hasse, Leah Knight, Danielle Berado, and Terese Jean Lund, "The Four P's of Purpose among College Bound Students: People, Propensity, Passion, Prosocial Benefits," *The Journal of Positive Psychology* 12, no. 3 (2017): 281–94.

19. Parks, *Big Questions, Worthy Dreams*, 128–31. In her discussion, she reserves mentors for older adolescents (seventeen and up), but I argue that younger adolescents benefit from these kinds of relationships as well.

20. Chap Clark, *Hurt: Inside the World of Today's Teenagers* (Grand Rapids, MI: Baker Academic, 2004). Clark reports that some adolescents assume that parents are only looking for a return on their investment.

21. That person does not always need to be a mature adult, but does need to be sufficiently older than the adolescent to offer perspective not available.

22. Lev S. Vygotsky, *Mind in Society: The Development of Higher Educational Processes* (Cambridge, MA: Harvard University Press, 1978), 86. "The level of potential development…under adult guidance or in collaboration with more capable peers."

23. Hans-Georg Gadamer, *Truth and Method*, 2nd rev. ed. (New York: Continuum, 1999), 302–7.

24. Gadamer, *Truth and Method*, 306.

25. Deborah Yurgelun-Todd, "Emotional and Cognitive Changes during Adolescence," *Current Opinion in Neurobiology* 17 (2007): 251–57. Research shows that younger adolescents consistently misinterpret the intentions of adults, but in time and with practice, they come to read the many and various cues.

26. Erikson, *Identity*, 128–30.

27. Kegan, *In Over Our Heads*, 47.

28. Kegan, *In Over Our Heads*, 43.

29. Sharon Daloz Parks, *Big Questions, Worthy Dreams*, 128–31.

30. Catherine Mowry LaCugna, *God for Us: The Trinity and Christian Life* (San Francisco: HarperSanFrancisco, 1991), 284.

31. LaCugna, *God for Us*, 299.

6. Rigging a Larger Boat

1. No sailboat can sail directly into the wind, but always at an angle to the oncoming wind. Boats with two sails can sail at a higher angle to the wind, thus enabling faster progress in that direction.

2. Standing rigging are those lines (stays and shrouds) that support the upright mast. The tension on them allows the masts to have both stability and flexibility when the boat is under sail. The higher the mast, the stronger the standing rigging needs to be to support it. As boats increase in size, the rigging becomes heavier and more complex so as to bear a greater load and sail in heavier weather. Very small boats do not have such rigging. Dave Franzel, *Sailing: The Basics* (Camden, ME: International Marine Publishing Company, 1985), 11–12.

Notes

3. The first major period was during infancy to age three. The field of neurobiology has been recently exploding. In some instances, the research is presented as a key for explaining all of life's mysteries or promoting educational methodology. This is not the tack I am taking here. My intent is to give the reader a basic sense of the dynamism and possibilities of this period of adolescence. A valuable resource on the topic is Laurence Steinberg, *Age of Opportunity: Lessons from the New Science of Adolescence* (Boston: Mariner Books, 2014).

4. These findings are from a body of research conducted over the past two decades. A leader in this work is Jay N. Giedd at the University of California, San Diego. Jay N. Giedd, Jonathan Blumenthal, Neal Jeffries, F.X. Castellanos, Hong Liu, Alex Zijdenbos, Tomáš Paus, Alan Evans, and Judith Rapoport, "Brain Development during Childhood and Adolescence: A Longitudinal MRI Study," *Nature Neuroscience* 2 (1999): 861–63; Sarah Johnson, Robert Blum, and Jay N. Giedd, "Adolescent Maturity and the Brain: The Promise and Pitfalls of Neuroscience Research in Adolescent Health Policy," *Journal of Adolescent Health* 45 (2009): 216–21; and Rhoshel Lenroot and Jay Giedd, "Brain Development in Children and Adolescents: Insights from Anatomic Magnetic Resonance Imaging," *Neuroscience and Biobehavioral Reviews* 30 (2006): 718–29.

5. Steinberg, *Age of Opportunity*, 23. Steinberg offers a good, nontechnical definition of brain plasticity.

6. Linda Spear, *The Behavioral Neuroscience of Adolescence* (New York: W.W. Norton, 2010), esp. chap. 8.

7. Lenroot and Giedd, "Brain Development in Children and Adolescents," 724–25.

8. This phrase is used by Jay Giedd in an interview for the *Frontline* program "Inside the Teenage Brain" (2002), accessed October 24, 2011, http://www.pbs.org/wgbh/pages/frontline/shows/teenbrain/.

9. Sherri C. Widen, "Children's Interpretation of Facial Expressions: The Long Path from Valence-Based to Specific Discrete Categories," Emotion Review 5 (2013): 72–77; Sherri C. Widen and J. A. Russell, "Children's Scripts for Social Emotions: Causes and Consequences Are More Central than Are Facial Expressions," *British Journal of Developmental Psychology* 28 (2010): 565–81; and Batja Mesquita and Michael Boiger, "Emotions in Context: A Sociodynamic Model of Emotions," *Emotion Review* 6 (2014): 298–302.

10. Deborah Yurgelun-Todd, "Emotional and Cognitive Changes during Adolescence," *Current Opinion in Neurobiology* 17 (2007): 251–57; Deborah Yurgelun-Todd and William Killgore, "Fear-Related Activity in the Prefrontal Cortex Increases with Age during Adolescence: A Preliminary fMRI Study," *Neuroscience Letters* 406 (2006): 194–99.

11. Lenroot and Giedd, "Brain Development in Children and Adolescents"; Jay Giedd, "The Teen Brain: Insights from Neuroimaging," *Journal of Adolescent Health* 42 (2008): 335–43.

12. Giedd, "The Teen Brain," 336.

13. For example, Christian educator Dean Blevins argues for a more nuanced appreciation of adolescent risk-taking, rather than simply concluding that they are unable to think logically and maturely. Dean Blevins, "Brains on Fire: Neuroscience and the Gift of Youth," *The Journal of Youth Ministry* 12 (2014). 7–24.

14. David Elkind, *All Grown Up and No Place to Go: Teenagers in Crisis*, rev. ed. (Cambridge, MA: Da Capo Press, 1998), 40.

15. A helpful discussion of the development of the "social self" among the early Pragmatist tradition, particularly on the role of self-consciousness, can be found in chapter 2 of James A. Holstein and Jaber F. Gubrium, *Sources of the Self: Narrative Identity in a Postmodern World* (New York: Oxford University Press, 2000).

16. Running rigging are those lines (ropes) by which sails are hoisted (halyards) and adjusted (sheets) when the boat is underway. Franzel, *Sailing*, 11.

17. Robert Kegan, *In Over Our Heads*, 21. Kegan builds off the work of Piaget, who previously identified this "cross-categorical" knowing as "formal operations." In both cases, it describes the ability for more abstract thought.

18. Kegan, *In Over Our Heads*, 25.

19. Kegan, *In Over Our Heads*, 38–42. Kegan makes an argument that those who may be classified as sociopaths in fact might be second-order knowers who are expected to understand and take on board concerns for others.

20. Eleanor Drago-Severson, *Becoming Adult Learners: Principles and Practices for Effective Development* (New York: Teachers College Press, 2004), 25.

21. Kegan, *In Over Our Heads*, 31.

22. Kegan, *In Over Our Heads*, 26.

23. As discussed earlier, research shows that adolescents frequently misread adult intention. Deborah Yurgelun-Todd summarizes these findings in "Interview Deborah Yurgelun-Todd," *Inside the Teenage Brain* (Boston: Frontline PBS, 2002), http://www.pbs.org/wgbh/pages/frontline/shows/teenbrain/interviews/todd.html.

24. Kegan, *In Over Our Heads*, 29, 32.

25. Kegan, *In Over Our Heads*, 18–19.

7. Learning to Serve as Crew

1. Robert Kegan, "What 'Form' Transforms? A Constructive-Developmental Approach to Transformative Learning," in *Learning as Transformation: Critical Perspectives on a Theory in Progress*, ed. Jack Mezirow (San Francisco: Jossey-Bass, 2000).

2. Jack Mezirow, *Transformative Dimensions of Adult Learning* (San Francisco: Jossey-Bass, 1991), 167–68.

3. Mezirow, *Transformative Dimensions of Adult Learning*, 168.

4. Robert Kegan, *In Over Our Heads: The Mental Demands of Modern Life* (Cambridge, MA: Harvard University Press, 1994). See a fuller discussion of Kegan's theory as it applies here in chapter 6.

5. Kegan, *In Over Our Heads*, 42.

6. Kegan, *In Over Our Heads*, 43. Kegan develops his idea of holding environments from Donald W. Winnicott, *The Maturational Processes and the Facilitating Environment* (New York: International University Press, 1965). Winnicott used the same term to refer only to the infant whose perception is embedded in the relationship with the caregiver. Kegan argues that humans are always socially embedded; however, one can disembed or individuate from one's "life-surround" so as to more clearly distinguish oneself from the environment. Kegan argues that this is the work of growth. Robert Kegan, *The Evolving Self: Problem and Process in Human Development* (Cambridge, MA: Harvard University Press, 1982), 116.

7. Kegan, *In Over Our Heads*, 17–18. David Elkind writes of the increased morbidity in adolescence as indicative of the increased stress and failure to meet that stress adequately. David Elkind, *All Grown Up and No Place to Go: Teenagers in Crisis*, rev. ed. (Cambridge, MA: Da Capo Press, 1998), 18–19. An additional source of stress comes from

the adolescent functioning in multiple relational contexts wherein they recognize that expectations in each are different and possibly contradictory.

8. The call for a balance of support and challenge coheres with the research on the success of differing parenting styles for "independent problem solving and critical thinking" as described by James Côté in "Identity Formation and Self-Development in Adolescence," in *Handbook of Adolescent Psychology*, ed. Richard Lerner and Laurence Steinberg (Hoboken, NJ: Wiley & Sons, 2009), 280–81.

9. This is a term used to indicate being on dry land, usually referring to boats in storage.

10. Ironically, the exhaustion may come from years of explaining to the same child when that child was too young to understand the explanation. Now when it is comprehendible, the parent may have had enough talk.

11. Elkind, *All Grown Up and No Place to Go*, 37–39.

12. There are mixed findings on the effects of overparenting, but they generally do point to the potential disadvantages for development of parents working to remove all impediments from the lives of adolescents. Jill Bradley-Geist and Julie B. Olson-Buchanan, "Helicopter Parents: An Examination of the Correlates of Over-Parenting of College Students," *Education + Training* 56 (2014): 314–28; and Chris Segrin, Alesia Woszidlo, Michelle Givertz, Amy Bauer, and Melissa Murphy, "The Association between Overparenting, Parent-Child Communication, and Entitlement and Adaptive Traits in Adult Children," *Family Relations* 61 (2012): 237–52.

13. Mezirow, *Transformative Dimensions of Adult Learning*, 169. Mezirow describes this as a shift in meaning perspectives. Once the perspective is reset, the information (meaning schemes) that populates the perspective begins to fall into place.

14. While it is beyond the scope of this chapter, research in "attachment theory" would open up an appraisal of patterns of relating with others seeking affirmation and trust. See John Bowlby, *A Secure Attachment: Parent-Child Attachment and Healthy Human Development* (New York: Basic Books, 1988); and Mary Ainsworth, "Attachments across the Life Span," *Bulletin of New York Academy of Medicine* 61, no. 9 (Nov 1985): 792–812. I am indebted to my colleagues Christopher Frechette and Melissa Kelley for directing me toward these

resources. Melissa Kelley, *Grief: Contemporary Theory and the Practice of Ministry* (Minneapolis, MN: Fortress Press, 2010).

15. "Skipper, the captain or master of a ship, but particularly applicable to smaller vessels." Peter Kemp, ed., *The Oxford Companion to Ships and the Sea* (Oxford: Oxford University Press, 1988), 807.

16. This concept is introduced in chapter 3, drawn from Karl Rahner, *Foundations of Christian Faith: An Introduction to the Idea of Christianity* (New York: Crossroad, 2000).

17. Edward Hahnenberg, *Awakening Vocation: A Theology of Christian Call* (Collegeville, MN: Michael Glazier, 2010), 130.

18. Erving Goffman, *The Presentation of Self in Everyday Life* (New York: Doubleday, 1959).

19. Smith described this as the kind of God he found prevalent among thirteen to seventeen-year-olds he studied. Christian Smith, *Soul Searching: The Religious and Spiritual Lives of American Teenagers* (New York: Oxford University Press, 2004).

20. Hahnenberg, *Awakening Vocation*, 131. A primary text Hahnenberg draws on for this discussion is Karl Rahner, *Foundations in Christian Faith: An Introduction to the Idea of Christianity*, trans. William V. Dych (New York: Crossroad, 1978).

21. Hahnenberg, *Awakening Vocation*, 131.

22. Hahnenberg, *Awakening Vocation*, 132.

23. Hahnenberg, *Awakening Vocation*, 132.

24. Obviously, to place God on the same horizon as others, and not the horizon itself, indicates that the adolescent does not recognize God as ultimate. It is not uncommon for the adolescent to recognize that God oversees religious things but not everything, and that something else is the source of all life.

25. Practical theologian James Loder recognizes that transformational experiences may first be perceived as threatening; he names them experiences of the "Void." James Loder, *The Transforming Moment: Understanding Convictional Experiences* (New York: Harper & Row, 1981), 79–83.

26. Hahnenberg, *Awakening Vocation*, 165.

27. Hahnenberg, *Awakening Vocation*, 132.

28. Hahnenberg, *Awakening Vocation*, 170.

29. Hahnenberg, *Awakening Vocation*, 177. Hahnenberg draws on two sources for Boeve: *God Interrupts History: Theology in a Time of Upheaval* (New York: Continuum, 2007); and *Interrupting Tradition:*

An Essay on Christian Faith in a Postmodern Context (Louvain: Peeters Press, 2003).

30. Hahnenberg, *Awakening Vocation*, 177.

31. Hahnenberg, *Awakening Vocation*, 178.

32. Hahnenberg, *Awakening Vocation*, 183–84.

33. *Interruption* as used by Hahnenberg reflects the interpretive process described by Gadamer, of preunderstanding, misunderstanding, and coming to a new understanding, discussed earlier. Hans-Georg Gadamer, *Truth and Method*, 2nd rev. ed. (New York: Continuum, 1999).

8. Sharing a Storied Horizon

1. Catherine LaCugna, *God with Us: The Trinity and Christian Life* (San Francisco: HarperSanFrancisco, 1991), 302. LaCugna's argument is explored more fully in chapter 4.

2. Hans-Georg Gadamer, *Truth and Method*, 2nd rev. ed. (New York: Continuum, 1999), 302.

3. Gadamer, *Truth and Method*, 302.

4. Belle Laing, Allison White, Angela DeSilva Mousseau, Alexandra Hasse, Leah Knight, Danielle Berado, and Terese Jean Lund, "The Four P's of Purpose among College Bound Students: People, Propensity, Passion, Prosocial Benefits," *The Journal of Positive Psychology* 12, no. 3 (2017): 291; Peter Scales, Peter Benson, and Marc Mannes, "The Contribution to Adolescent Well-Being Made by Non-family Adults: An Examination of Developmental Assets as Contexts and Processes," *Journal of Community Psychology* 34 (2006): 410–13.

5. Liang et al., "The Four P's of Purpose among College Bound Students," 291.

6. Edward Hahnenberg, *Awakening Vocation: A Theology of Christian Call* (Collegeville, MN: Liturgical Press, 2010), 131.

7. James W. Fowler, *Stages of Faith: The Psychology of Human Development and the Quest of Meaning* (San Francisco, CA: Harper & Row, 1981), 136.

8. Fowler, *Stages of Faith*, 139.

9. Fowler, *Stages of Faith*, 143.

10. James W. Fowler, *Becoming Adult, Becoming Christian: Adult Development and Christian Faith* (San Francisco, CA: Jossey-Bass, 2000), 45–46.

11. The Vatican II Dogmatic Constitution on Divine Revelation, *Dei Verbum*, affirms "the books of Scripture must be acknowledged as teaching firmly, faithfully, and without error that truth which God wanted put into the sacred writings for the sake of our salvation" (no. 11). As explained in the translation's footnote, "The Bible was not written in order to teach the natural sciences, nor to give information on merely political history. It treats of these (and all other subjects) only insofar as they are involved in matters concerning salvation. It is only in this respect that the veracity of God and the inerrancy of the inspired writers are engaged." "Dei Verbum," *The Documents of Vatican II*, ed. Walter Abbot, trans. Joseph Gallagher (New York: Guild Press, 1966), 119n31.

12. Fowler, *Becoming Adult, Becoming Christian*, 45. See also Christian Smith, *Soul Searching: The Religious and Spiritual Lives of American Teenagers* (New York: Oxford University Press, 2009).

13. Theologian Nicholas Lash creates a valuable argument about the difference between scientific and theological argument and claims. He bemoans the effort of religious people to try to argue science from theological texts. Likewise, he challenges scientists who dismiss religious belief because it is bad science. Nicholas Lash, *Believing Three Ways in One God: A Reading of the Apostles' Creed* (Notre Dame, IN: University of Notre Dame Press, 1992).

14. Edward Farley, *Deep Symbols: Their Postmodern Effacement and Reclamation* (Valley Forge, PA: Trinity Press International, 1996). Farley argues that Christian symbols have lost their power because they have become disconnected from the narratives and communities that gave them meaning and power.

15. Fowler, *Becoming Adult, Becoming Christian*, 47.

16. Fowler, *Becoming Adult, Becoming Christian*, 47.

17. Fowler, *Becoming Adult, Becoming Christian*, 47.

18. Hahnenberg, *Awakening Vocation*, 167.

19. Alasdair MacIntyre, *After Virtue: A Study in Moral Theory*, 2nd ed. (Notre Dame, IN: University of Notre Dame Press, 1984), 216.

20. MacIntyre, *After Virtue*, 216.

21. Hahnenberg, *Awakening Vocation*, 152.

22. Hahnenberg, *Awakening Vocation*, 160.

23. Thomas H. Groome, *Will There Be Faith: A New Vision for Educating and Growing Disciples* (New York: HarperCollins, 2011), 262. Groome summarizes his *shared Christian praxis approach* of religious education as "bringing life to Faith and Faith to life." His is a helpful approach for engaging adolescents with Christian narratives.

24. MacIntyre, *After Virtue*, 206.

25. MacIntyre, *After Virtue*, 213.

26. MacIntyre, *After Virtue*, 214.

27. MacIntyre, *After Virtue*, 216.

28. Ernesto Valiente, "Oscar Romero: Renewed by the Spirit," in *The Holy Spirit: Setting the World on Fire*, eds. Richard Lennan and Nancy Pineda-Madrid (New York: Paulist Press, 2017).

29. MacIntyre, *After Virtue*, 204.

30. Christian Smith, *Lost in Transition: The Dark Side of Emerging Adulthood* (New York: Oxford University Press, 2011). Smith notes a lack of integrity or absence of a moral framework among adolescents he studied.

31. See Pope Paul VI, *Dignitatis Humanae*, Declaration on Religious Freedom (December 7, 1965), no. 2, http://www.vatican.va/archive/hist_councils/ii_vatican_council/documents/vat-ii_decl_19651207_dignitatis-humanae_en.html.

32. Simone Campbell, *The Nun on the Bus: How All of Us Can Create Hope, Change, and Community* (New York: HarperCollins, 2014).

33. MacIntyre, *After Virtue*, 215–16. Sociologists Holstein and Gubrium make a similar argument: The self is "a moral entity because, in part, it propels itself on its own and makes choices. In a postmodern world, the self's story forges ahead, but also follows in its own wake." James Holstein and Jaber Gubrium, *The Self We Live By: Narrative Identity in a Postmodern World* (New York: Oxford University Press, 2000), 215.

34. Elizabeth Johnson, *Friends of God and Prophets: A Feminist Theological Reading of the Communion of Saints* (New York: Continuum, 1999), 212.

9. Learning to Sail from Sailors

1. United States Conference of Catholic Bishops, *Renewing the Vision: A Framework for Catholic Youth Ministry* (Washington, DC:

Notes

USCCB, 1997); and *Sons and Daughters of Light: A Pastoral Plan for Ministry with Young Adults* (Washington, DC: USCCB, 1997). For the U.S. Catholic Church, these hopes are most clearly expressed in these two documents.

2. Congregation for the Clergy, *General Directory for Catechesis* (Washington, DC: United States Catholic Conference, 1997), §30.

3. Robert Kegan, *The Evolving Self: Problem and Process in Human Development* (Cambridge, MA: Harvard University Press, 1994), 116; and Kegan, *In Over Our Heads*, 43.

4. Alasdair MacIntyre, *After Virtue: A Study in Moral Theory*, 2nd ed. (Notre Dame, IN: University of Notre Dame Press, 1984), 191.

5. Edward Hahnenberg, *Awakening Vocation: A Theology of Christian Call* (Collegeville, MN: Liturgical Press, 2010), 165.

6. Note the discussion of grace in chapters 3 and 7.

7. MacIntyre, *After Virtue*, 188.

8. Hans-Georg Gadamer, *Truth and Method*, 2nd rev. ed., trans. Joel Weinsheimer and Donald Marshall (New York: Crossroads, 1999), 270. Gadamer described prejudice as "judgment rendered before."

9. Gadamer, *Truth and Method*, 269.

10. Gadamer, *Truth and Method*, 362.

11. Theresa O'Keefe, "Relationships across the Divide: An Instigator of Transformation," *Studies in Christian-Jewish Relations* 5 (2010): 1–22, doi.org/10.6017/scjr.v5i1.1553. I report two study findings. When given the opportunity for conversation across a difference, participants were able to see themselves with greater clarity and to recognize presumptions they held about the other.

12. Theresa O'Keefe, "Learning to Talk: Conversation across Religious Difference," *Religious Education* 104 (2009): 197–213. I report that when given the opportunity for conversation across an acknowledged difference, participants presumed it would not be possible and so were inclined to remain silent. Constructive conversation ensued when prompted by safety and good direction.

13. Nicholas Burbules, *Dialogue in Teaching: Theory and Practice* (New York: Teachers College Press, 1993), 41.

14. Burbules, *Dialogue in Teaching*, 43.

15. Burbules, *Dialogue in Teaching*, 43.

16. Hahnenberg, *Awakening Vocation*, 208. Hahnenberg draws from Ellacuría's "The Historicity of Christian Salvation," in *Mysterium Liberationis: Fundamental Concepts of Liberation Theology*,

161

eds. Ignacio Ellacuría and Jon Sobrino, trans. Margaret Wilde (Mary-knoll, NY: Orbis, 1993), among other sources.

17. Hahnenberg, *Awakening Vocation*, 208.

18. Hahnenberg, *Awakening Vocation*, 211.

19. Hahnenberg, *Awakening Vocation*, 213.

20. MacIntyre, *After Virtue*, 191.

21. Fred P. Edie, *Book, Bath, Table, and Time: Christian Worship as Source and Resource for Youth Ministry* (Cleveland, OH: Pilgrim Press, 2007), 6.

22. David White, *Practicing Discernment with Youth: A Transformative Youth Ministry Approach* (Cleveland, OH: Pilgrim Press, 2005), 46. White also critiques the efforts to compete with wider cultural forces in the attraction and entertainment of youth. That is a losing game and the wrong game for the church to be playing.

23. Charles Taylor, *The Ethics of Authenticity* (Cambridge MA: Harvard University Press, 1991), 27–29.

24. A caveat must be made here. Since adolescents are seeking the attention of older persons but are unskilled at forming such relationships, they may be susceptible to the advances of those adults who mean them harm, especially if that adult appears to the adolescent as the only adult taking notice of the adolescent. This makes the cultivation of a network of robust relationships within a community even more important.

25. An important example for the early twenty-first century are people who experience gender fluidity or same-sex attraction but hide it from significant others for fear of rejection and reprisal.

26. Kegan, *In Over Our Heads*, 43.

27. Sharon Daloz Parks, *Big Questions, Worthy Dreams: Mentoring Young Adults in Their Search for Meaning, Purpose, and Faith* (San Francisco, CA: Jossey-Bass, 2000), 128–31.

28. The Volvo Ocean 65 is a sixty-five-foot sloop, designed especially for this race, and raced by a team of eight.

29. Elizabeth Johnson, *Friends of God and Prophets: A Feminist Theological Reading of the Communion of Saints* (New York, NY: Continuum, 1999), 219.

30. Johnson, *Friends of God and Prophets*, 219.

Selected Bibliography

Arnett, Jeffrey. *Emerging Adulthood: The Winding Road from the Late Teens to the Twenties.* New York: Oxford University Press, 2004.

Beaudoin, Tom. *Consuming Faith: Integrating Who We Are with What We Buy.* Lanham, MD: Sheed & Ward, 2003.

Bellah, Robert, Richard Madsen, William Sullivan, Ann Swidler, and Steven Tipton. *Habits of the Heart: Individualism and Commitment in American Life.* Berkeley, CA: University of California Press, 2008.

Blevins, Dean. "Brains on Fire: Neuroscience and the Gift of Youth." *The Journal of Youth Ministry* 12 (2014): 7–24.

boyd, danah. *It's Complicated: The Social Lives of Networked Teens.* New Haven, CT: Yale University Press, 2014.

Buckingham, David, ed. *Youth, Identity and Digital Media.* Cambridge, MA: MIT Press, 2008.

Burbles, Nicholas. *Dialogue in Teaching: Theory and Practice.* New York: Teachers College Press, 1993.

Clark, Chap. *Hurt: Inside the World of Today's Teenagers.* Grand Rapids, MI: Baker Academic, 2004.

Congregation for the Clergy. *General Directory for Catechesis.* Washington, DC: United States Catholic Conference, 1997.

Côté, James. "Identity Formation and Self-Development in Adolescence." In *Handbook of Adolescent Psychology*, edited by Richard Lerner and Laurence Steinberg, 266–302. Hoboken, NJ: Wiley & Sons, 2009.

Damon, William. *The Path to Purpose: How Young People Find Their Calling in Life.* New York: Free Press, 2008.

Drago-Severson, Eleanor. *Becoming Adult Learners: Principles and Practices for Effective Development.* New York: Teachers College Press, 2004.

Eck, Diana. *A New Religious America: How a "Christian Country" Has become the World's Most Religiously Diverse Nation.* San Francisco: HarperSanFrancisco, 2002.

Edie, Fred P. *Book, Bath, Table, and Time: Christian Worship as Source and Resource for Youth Ministry.* Cleveland, OH: Pilgrim Press, 2007.

Elkind, David. *All Grown Up and No Place to Go: Teenagers in Crisis.* Rev. ed. Cambridge, MA: De Capo Press, 1998.

Epstein, Robert. *The Case against Adolescence: Rediscovering the Adult in Every Teen.* Sanger, CA: Quill Driver Books, 2007.

Erikson, Erik. *Identity: Youth and Crisis.* New York: W.W. Norton & Co., 1968.

Farley, Edward. *Deep Symbols: Their Postmodern Effacement and Reclamation.* Valley Forge, PA: Trinity Press International, 1996.

Fowler, James W. *Becoming Adult, Becoming Christian: Adult Development and Christian Faith.* San Francisco, CA: Jossey-Bass, 2000.

———. *Stages of Faith: The Psychology of Human Development and the Quest of Meaning.* San Francisco, CA: Harper & Row, 1981.

Franzel, Dave. *Sailing: The Basics.* Camden, ME: International Marine Publishing Company, 1985.

Freitas, Donna. *Sex and the Soul: Juggling Sexuality, Spirituality, Romance and Religion on America's College Campus.* New York: Oxford University Press, 2008.

Gadamer, Hans-Georg. *Truth and Method.* 2nd rev. ed. New York: Continuum, 1999.

Giedd, Jay N., Jonathan Blumenthal, Neal Jeffries, F. X. Castellanos, Hong Liu, Alex Zijdenbos, Tomáš Paus, Alan Evans, and Judith Rapoport. "Brain Development during Childhood and Adolescence: A Longitudinal MRI Study." *Nature Neuroscience* 2 (1999): 861–63.

Giedd, Jay. "The Teen Brain: Insights from Neuroimaging." *Journal of Adolescent Health* 42 (2008): 335–43.

Goffman, Erving. *The Presentation of Self in Everyday Life.* New York: Doubleday, 1959.

Groome, Thomas H. *Will There Be Faith: A New Vision for Educating and Growing Disciples.* New York: HarperCollins, 2011.

Selected Bibliography

Hahnenberg, Edward. *Awakening Vocation: A Theology of Christian Call.* Collegeville, MN: Liturgical Press, 2010.

Hanawalt, Barbara A. *Growing Up in Medieval London: The Experience of Childhood in History.* New York: Oxford University Press, 1993.

Herlihy, David. *Women, Family and Society in Medieval Europe: Historical Essays, 1978-1991.* Providence, RI: Berghahn Books, 1995.

Holstein, James, and Jaber Gubrim. *The Self We Live By: Narrative Identity in a Postmodern World.* New York: Oxford University Press, 1999.

Johnson, Elizabeth A. *Friends of God and Prophets: A Feminist Theological Reading of the Communion of Saints.* New York: Continuum, 1999.

Johnson, Sarah, Robert Blum, and Jay N. Giedd. "Adolescent Maturity and the Brain: The Promise and Pitfalls of Neuroscience Research in Adolescent Health Policy." *Journal of Adolescent Health* 45 (2009): 216–21.

Kegan, Robert. *The Evolving Self: Problem and Process in Human Development.* Cambridge, MA: Harvard University Press, 1982.

———. *In Over Our Heads: The Mental Demands of Modern Life.* Cambridge MA: Harvard University Press, 1994.

Kett, Joseph. *Rites of Passage: Adolescence in America 1790 to the Present.* New York: Basic Books, 1977.

Kimmel, Michael. *Guyland: The Perilous World Where Boys Become Men.* New York: HarperCollins, 2008.

Kirgiss, Crystal. *In Search of Adolescence: A New Look at an Old Idea.* San Diego, CA: The Youth Cartel, 2015.

LaCugna, Catherine Mowry. *God for Us: The Trinity and Christian Life.* San Francisco: HarperSanFrancisco, 1991.

Laing, Belle, Allison White, Angela DeSilva Mouseau, Alexandra Hasse, Leah Knight, Danielle Berado, and Terese Jean Lund. "The Four P's of Purpose among College Bound Students: People, Propensity, Passion, Prosocial Benefits." *The Journal of Positive Psychology* 12 (2017): 281–94.

Lash, Nicholas. *Believing Three Ways in One God: A Reading of the Apostles' Creed.* Notre Dame, IN: University of Notre Dame Press, 1992.

Lenhart, Amanda. "Teens, Social Media, and Technology Overview 2015." *Pew Research Center: Internet, Science, and Tech.* April 9,

2015. http://www.pewinternet.org/2015/04/09/teens-social-media -technology-2015/.

Lennan, Richard, and Nancy Pineda-Madrid, eds. *The Holy Spirit: Setting the World on Fire*. New York: Paulist Press, 2017.

Lenroot, Rhoshel, and Jay Giedd. "Brain Development in Children and Adolescents: Insights from Anatomic Magnetic Resonance Imaging." *Neuroscience and Biobehavioral Reviews* 30 (2006): 718–29.

Loder, James. *The Transforming Moment: Understanding Convictional Experiences*. New York: Harper & Row, 1981.

MacIntyre, Alasdair. *After Virtue: A Study in Moral Theory*. 2nd ed. Notre Dame, IN: University of Notre Dame Press, 1984.

Mesquita, Batja, and Michael Boiger. "Emotions in Context: A Sociodynamic Model of Emotions." *Emotion Review* 6 (2014): 298–302.

Mezirow, Jack. *Transformative Dimensions of Adult Learning*. San Francisco: Jossey-Bass, 1991.

———, ed. *Learning as Transformation: Critical Perspectives on a Theory in Progress*. San Francisco: Jossey-Bass, 2000.

Miller, Vincent. *Consuming Religion: Christian Faith and Practice in a Consumer Culture*. New York: Continuum, 2003.

Oberle, Eva, Kimberly Schonert-Reichl, and Bruno Zumbo. "Life Satisfaction in Early Adolescence: Personal, Neighborhood, School, Family, and Peer Influences." *Journal of Youth and Adolescence* 40 (2011): 889–901.

O'Keefe, Theresa. "Companioning Adolescents into Adulthood: Schools as Communities of Care and Growth." In *Education Matters: Reading in Pastoral Care for School Chaplains, Guidance Counsellors and Teachers*, edited by James O'Higgins Norman, 132–46. Dublin, Ireland: Veritas Publications, 2014.

———. "Growing Up Alone: The New Normal of Isolation in Adolescents," *The Journal of Youth Ministry* 13 (2014): 63–84.

———. "Learning to Talk: Conversation across Religious Difference." *Religious Education*, 104 (2009): 197–213.

———. "Relationships across the Divide: An Instigator of Transformation." *Studies in Christian-Jewish Relations* 5 (2010): 1–22.

Orme, Nicholas. *Medieval Children*. New Haven, CT: Yale University Press, 2001.

Selected Bibliography

————. *Medieval Schools: From Roman Britain to Renaissance England.* New Haven, CT: Yale University Press, 2006.

Parks, Sharon Daloz. *Big Questions, Worthy Dreams: Mentoring Young Adults in Their Search for Meaning, Purpose, and Faith.* San Francisco: Jossey-Bass, 2000.

Putnam, Robert. *Bowling Alone: The Collapse and Revival of American Community.* New York: Simon & Schuster, 2000.

Rahner, Karl. *Foundations of Christian Faith: An Introduction to the Idea of Christianity.* New York: Crossroads, 1978.

Rainie, Lee, and Barry Wellman. *Networked: The New Social Operating System.* Cambridge, MA: MIT Press, 2012.

Rausch, Thomas. *Being Catholic in a Culture of Choice.* Collegeville, MN: Liturgical Press, 2006.

Scales, Peter C., Peter L. Benson, and Mark Mannes. "The Contribution to Adolescent Well-Being Made by Nonfamily Adults: An Examination of Developmental Assets as Contexts and Processes." *Journal of Community Psychology* 34 (2006): 401–13.

Schor, Juliet. *Born to Buy: The Commercialized Child and the New Consumer Culture.* New York: Scribner, 2004.

————. *The Overspent American: Why We Want What We Don't Need.* New York: Basic Books, 1998.

Smith, Christian, and Melinda Lundquist Denton. *Soul Searching: The Religious and Spiritual Lives of American Teenagers.* New York: Oxford University Press, 2004.

Smith, Christian, Kari Christoffersen, Hilary Davidson, and Patricia Snell Herzog. *Lost in Transition: The Dark Side of Emerging Adulthood.* New York: Oxford University Press, 2011.

Smith, Christian, Kyle Longest, Jonathan Hill, and Kari Christoffersen. *Young Catholic America: Emerging Adults In, Out of, and Gone from the Church.* New York: Oxford University Press, 2014.

Spear, Linda P. *The Behavioral Neuroscience of Adolescence.* New York: W.W. Norton, 2010.

Steinberg, Laurence. *The Age of Opportunity: Lessons from the New Science of Adolescence.* Boston: Mariner Books, 2014.

Taylor, Charles. *The Ethics of Authenticity.* Cambridge MA: Harvard University Press, 1991.

————. *Sources of the Self: The Making of the Modern Identity.* Cambridge, MA: Harvard University Press, 1989.

Turkle, Sherry. *Alone Together: Why We Expect More from Technology and Less from Each Other.* New York: Basic Books, 2011.
———. *Reclaiming Conversation: The Power of Talk in a Digital Age.* New York: Penguin Press, 2015.
United States Conference of Catholic Bishops. *Renewing the Vision: A Framework for Catholic Youth Ministry.* Washington, DC: USCCB, Inc., 1997.
———. *Sons and Daughters of Light: A Pastoral Plan for Ministry with Young Adults.* Washington, DC: USCCB, Inc., 1997.
Vygotsky, Lev S. *Mind in Society: The Development of Higher Educational Processes.* Cambridge MA: Harvard University Press, 1978.
Waters, Mary C., Patrick J. Carr, Maria J. Kefalas, and Jennifer Holdaway, eds. *Coming of Age in America: The Transition to Adulthood in the Twenty-First Century.* Berkley, CA: University of California Press, 2011.
White, David. *Practicing Discernment with Youth: A Transformative Youth Ministry Approach.* Cleveland, OH: The Pilgrim Press, 2005.
Widen, Sherri C. "Children's Interpretation of Facial Expressions: The Long Path from Valence-Based to Specific Discrete Categories." *Emotion Review* 5 (2013): 72–77.
Widen, Sherri C., and J. A. Russell. "Children's Scripts for Social Emotions: Causes and Consequences Are More Central than Are Facial Expressions." *British Journal of Developmental Psychology* 28 (2010): 565–81.
Yurgelun-Todd, Deborah. "Emotional and Cognitive Changes during Adolescence." *Current Opinion in Neurobiology* 17 (2007): 251–57.
Yurgelen-Todd, Deborah, and William Killgore. "Fear-Related Activity in the Prefrontal Cortex Increases with Age during Adolescence: A Preliminary fMRI Study." *Neuroscience Letters* 406 (2006): 194–99.
Zizioulas, John D. *Being as Communion: Studies in Personhood and the Church.* Crestwood, NY: St. Vladimir's Seminary Press, 2002.
———. "The Doctrine of the Holy Trinity: The Significance of the Cappadocian Contribution." In *Trinitarian Theology Today: Essays on Divine Being and Act,* edited by Christoph Schwöbel, 44–60. Edinburgh: T&T Clark, 1995.

Index

Index